SARAH CHILDRESS POLK

MVFOL

Sarah Childress Polk

A Biography of the Remarkable First Lady

BY
JOHN REED BUMGARNER

with a foreword by
JUDY CHEATHAM *and* GEORGE CHEATHAM

McFarland & Company, Inc., Publishers
Jefferson, North Carolina, and London

ALSO BY JOHN REED BUMGARNER

*Parade of the Dead: A U.S. Army Physician's Memoir
of Imprisonment by the Japanese, 1942–1945*
(McFarland, 1995)

*The Health of the Presidents: The 41 United States Presidents
Through 1993 from a Physician's Point of View*
(McFarland, 1994)

Front cover/frontispiece: Portrait of Sarah Childress Polk by
George E. A. Healy (1846); photograph of Polk Place in
Nashville, Tennessee (portrait and photograph courtesy of the
James K. Polk Memorial Association, Columbia, Tennessee)

British Library Cataloguing-in-Publication data are available

Library of Congress Cataloguing-in-Publication Data

ISBN 0-7864-0366-7 (sewn softcover : 50# alkaline paper) ∞

Manufactured in the United States of America

*McFarland & Company, Inc., Publishers
Box 611, Jefferson, North Carolina 28640*

I wish to dedicate this, my third book,
to my grandchildren, Sylvan, Oren, Bob, and Jimmy

Acknowledgments

No one can write anything of a biographical nature without considerable help from reference librarians. I recognize Elizabeth Herman of the Greensboro City Library and Susan Younts of the University of North Carolina Library who have been indispensable in helping me to find reference materials. I also recognize the very valuable assistance of Carol Rawleigh in editing all the material in the manuscript.

Contents

Foreword

Since his retirement from the practice of medicine in 1985, John Bumgarner has — inspirationally, we think — transformed himself into a professional writer. We are honored to have been associated with this blossoming second career, having edited his first two books, *The Health of the Presidents* (McFarland, 1994) and *Parade of the Dead* (McFarland, 1995). The earlier book both reflects Bumgarner's abiding interest in medicine and raises serious questions about the political implications of presidential health. The later book relates in moving detail his formative experiences as an army physician in the Philippines and as a prisoner of war captured by the Japanese during the fall of Bataan.

Bumgarner's third book, *Sarah Childress Polk*, is less personal but perhaps more timely. The career of Hillary Rodham Clinton has raised questions about the role and importance of the first lady. In the context of this ongoing debate, the life of Sarah Polk certainly merits the close scrutiny provided here. As Bumgarner insightfully reveals, the well-educated, shrewdly ambitious, and politically savvy first lady is not unique to the twentieth century.

JUDY CHEATHAM
GEORGE CHEATHAM

Preface

My choice to write about Mrs. Polk arose in an unusual way. While working on my first book, *The Health of the Presidents*, I found James Knox Polk to have some fascinating illnesses, and for that reason I decided to write a biography on the eleventh president. However, on probing further, I found that Charles Sellers had already written a detailed, two-volume biography. I also found that Polk was not nearly as interesting as his wife, Sarah Childress Polk. For this reason, I chose Mrs. Polk as my subject. Throughout my extensive research, using the available information on Mrs. Polk, I found that she was indeed a most remarkable lady.

Chapter 1

There have been strong women in the White House other than Sarah Childress Polk: Edith Wilson, Eleanor Roosevelt, and Hillary Rodham Clinton, to name a few. But none exerted their influence politically in the manner of Sarah Polk. Sarah's influence was exerted in an unobtrusive way. Eleanor Roosevelt was gone so much from the White House on behalf of her own agenda that one of her own children complained that she was neither a good wife nor a good mother. Hillary Rodham Clinton does indeed exert a lot of influence, but it would be difficult to say that her political presence is unobtrusive. In only a few instances did Sarah let her strength and influence show. She was always most eager to see that her husband was in the forefront in every respect. Other first ladies were perhaps forceful in running their own households and contending with the social life of Washington, but not one of them was effective in the same way that Sarah proved to be when she lived in the executive mansion.

Sarah Childress Polk was born September 4, 1803, in Murfreesboro, Tennessee. She was the third of six children born to Elizabeth Whitsett and Joel Childress, a planter. The first child was Anderson, born in 1799, followed by Susan, Sarah, Benjamin, John Whitsett, and Elizabeth. Two of the children, Benjamin and Elizabeth, died early of a febrile illness. The nature of the illness is not known and, since there is no existing description of the condition, it is possible only to surmise on the cause. Malaria, typhoid, and dysentery were widespread at that time; and it is known that whole families and at times whole communities were wiped out by the mysterious "milk fever." This illness was caused by drinking milk from a cow that had eaten the toxic white snakeroot.

Joel Childress and his family moved several times. They first lived in western North Carolina and then moved to Sumner County, Tennessee. When Sarah was five, the family moved again to Rutherford County, Tennessee. The Childress family undoubtedly was happy and

15

well adjusted. The father was a wealthy man whose thinking was beyond his time. In the early nineteenth century the emphasis in a family was on the education of sons. Even among the wealthy, daughters were not considered worthy of more than a basic education. Sarah's father expended much effort and a great deal of money to secure the best education possible for Sarah and Susan, and had he not died early in their development, he would almost certainly have made it possible for them to have gone to college.

At that time the education of females was in the hands of parents or at subscription schools, which taught only the three R's. Some of these schools, referred to as "old field schools," depended entirely on the interest and contributions of a local community. The Childress girls were sent to the finest schools available at that time. Sarah and Susan went as far as possible in the common school along with their brothers. After the common school, they were given tutelage by Samuel Black at the Bradley Academy at Murfreesboro. This was a boys' school, but Sarah and Susan were tutored privately after the regular school hours were over. They rode to their classes on their ponies, and after the lessons were over, they would return home with their brother Anderson as escort.

There are accounts that seek to prove that it was at the academy where Sarah first met James Knox Polk. One biographer of Polk says that it is almost certain that the two, who both attended Bradley Academy, had met there, at least casually.[1]

After being tutored at Bradley Academy, Susan and Sarah were sent to a fashionable school in Nashville, Tennessee, where they were taught social graces and piano, among other things. Nashville was by then a city with a few paved streets and a theater.[2] While at Abercrombie's Boarding School, the young ladies roomed with the family of Colonel Butler, who was connected with the school. Among their friends and classmates were their cousins, Matilda and Elizabeth Childress, the daughters of Judge John Childress. Susan and Sarah were frequent visitors in the judge's home, where Andrew Jackson, a friend of the judge, was often present as a guest.[3]

Here Sarah and Susan developed a very friendly relationship with General Jackson, the man who was to play the dominant role in furthering the political career of James Polk. The girls were said to have enjoyed hearing Andy talk about his warfare with the Indians.[4]

Sarah's father was a man of wealth and prominence. Before

Murfreesboro became the state capital, Major Childress had moved his family out of town to a plantation, where he and Mrs. Childress did much entertaining of lawyers and judges. The dress uniform worn by Andrew Jackson at New Salem, which cost over $500, had been given to him by Joel Childress.[5] This early relationship was to continue as the Jackson and Polk fortunes intertwined.

For Southern girls in the latter part of the eighteenth and the beginning of the nineteenth century the opportunities to receive an education beyond the most rudimentary were almost nonexistent. During the years following the American Revolution, academies for young males were relatively common in the South. These schools, which professed to instruct young men in the elements of language and science, were essentially prep schools for the colleges and universities of higher education. Parents who were desirous that their daughters, too, have a better education eagerly sought a place for them at the Moravian Female Academy in Salem, North Carolina.[6]

The little town of Salem was founded by the Society of the United Brethren, and under the direction of Count Zinzendorf, the female academy was founded at Salem in 1772 under the charge of the pious Moravian brothers.[7]

Joel Childress was anxious that his children should receive the best education possible. While Anderson was at the University of North Carolina at Chapel Hill, Sarah and Susan were sent to the Moravian Female Academy. Accompanied by Anderson and a slave, they journeyed on horseback over 500 miles from Murfreesboro to Salem. The trip took over a month, and both girls, as a parting gift, received a French gold piece from their father. This was a louis d'or, which Sarah prized for the rest of her life. Each night on the trip from Murfreesboro to Salem was spent at a hospitable farmhouse. We begin to get some idea about what a resolute and determined woman Sarah was to have endured such an arduous adventure as riding horseback for 500 miles. The academy had an arrangement with a local agency to purchase horses from students who arrived on horseback, and the revenue could be applied toward the tuition and other expenses.

Today Salem College has a special room on campus where numerous relics of the institution's past are preserved. In that room may be found saddles formerly belonging to students at the academy, but which were abandoned at the end of the long trip.[8] Salem College has very carefully preserved its past. Ledgers, which are as old as the academy,

The original building of the Moravian Female Academy (sketch by Doris Hayes; courtesy of the artist).

are thick and yellow with age. An entry in the general ledger on May 5, 1817 (the day of Sarah's matriculation), shows that Salem Academy received cash from Joel Childress amounting to $37.50, which was credited to Sarah's account. The ledger for 1817, the year of Sarah's attendance, has been lost, but the ledgers for each year were about the same with regard to the items entered. The detailed entries for 1819, two years after Sarah's attendance, were made in beautiful script and concern the expenditures of a teenage girl about Sarah's age. The items in the account book show how a teenage girl spent her money at the academy.

Sarah Childress
    Contra

1817

May 5   By cash rec. of Joel Childress Credit
          for James Childress   37.50
          Transferred to Book 5 — fol. 13

1819

Nov. 9   To one quarter advance commencing
          this day and ending the 9 February 1820 —

	Board and Tuition	24.00
	Washing 4.00, Music 3.00, fine 33.00	
	needlework 2.00	9.00
	To one Drawing book, pencil and rubber .64 (blank book .13)	.77
10	To ¼ yd Satin .50, 1.16 sk. Embr. silk	10.44
	floss cotton 06	11.00
27	To 2 yd calico .80 thread 03.83	12.60
Dec. 6	1 pr shoes 1.50	
14	To Postage 1 letter .18½, blankbook .10	
Dec. 25	To sundry Christmas expenses 1.00	2.50
	1 pr. shoes 1.50	
Mar. 14 1820		
	To music book .75, painting paper .10	.85
	To 3 yds gingham 1.38 tape .03	1.86
	medicine .45	
	To 2 blank books, sundry stationery & colours .39	3.10

Postage 2 letters .37

1 pr. stockings .80[9]

The academy was described as a plain building of two stories placed on a high ridge. The grounds were shaded by large oaks and hickories.[10] The subjects studied at the academy at that time included English grammar, Bible history, Greek and Roman literature, and sewing.[11] The study of foreign languages or science is not mentioned. Sarah became an avid reader and learned something about geography, music, and drawing.[12] This education was beyond that provided by most finishing schools that trained young girls to become homemakers.

The Moravian Female Academy was considered large for its time, with 150–200 students. During the Christmas season, teachers and students turned their attention to activities that emphasized the nativity. When New Year's Eve was celebrated in the chapel, all of the young ladies wore white lace caps. The older girls wore pink ribbons in their caps while the younger ones wore cherry-colored ribbons in theirs. The caps were the school's uniforms. The meeting was followed with a midnight watch, and later a New Year's sermon was preached.[13]

Surviving samples of needlework done by students attest to the excellence of the Moravian needlework. There survive several "mourning pieces," usually worn by mourners beside the grave of a deceased loved one. Among these is a mourning embroidery done by Sarah Childress in 1817 and 1818.

Part of Salem College lore concerns itself with a possible encounter between Sarah Childress and James Polk at the Moravian Female Academy. This meeting is presumed to have occurred in the living room of the inspector's house. Indeed, such a meeting was possible. Polk had been a classmate of Anderson Childress at a private academy in Murfreesboro. However, James was 21 and Sarah 14. The possibility of more than a courtesy call seems remote, for James was deeply and seriously involved in the study of law at the University of North Carolina.[14]

Sarah and Susan were to remain at the Moravian Female Academy for only a year. In August 1819 they were called home due to the death of their father, and their formal education was terminated.[15] Anderson Childress, Sarah's older brother, brought the news to the girls that their father had died. Anderson spoke in a solemn tone when he said, "Papa has had a serious illness. He is gone."[16]

As soon as Sarah and Susan got the news, and while trying to contain their grief, they began hurriedly to pack for their return home. Their trip to Murfreesboro by stagecoach required a week, not as much time as their earlier horseback ride to North Carolina. They interrupted their passage only long enough to replace the tired horses and to eat. The excursion was far from a pleasant one. Struggling with their grief, they were miserable from the hot and humid August days, the dusty roads, and biting insects. The road was bumpy and deeply grooved, and they were jostled and jolted to such a degree that they were unable to sleep. They arrived in Murfreesboro tired, miserable, and grief stricken.

Their father had already been buried by the time they reached home, but the funeral rites were delayed until all the family could be together to pay their respects. Sarah's brother, Anderson, delayed his return to the University of North Carolina until he could place a tombstone at his father's grave. The inscription was as follows: "Joel Childress, born March 22, 1777, died, August 19, 1819."[17] Joel Childress, a wealthy merchant, plantation owner, and slaveholder, left his family well provided. Each child became heir to one-fourth of this fortune, which was left in trust for them.[18]

Chapter 2

The last will and testament of Joel Childress, clear and detailed, reads as follows:

I, Joel Childress of Rutherford County in the state of Tennessee, being infirm of body, but of sound mind and memory, do by these presents make, constitute, and ordain that this, my last will and testament hereby revoking all others hereto made by me.

Viz: I recommend my body to the dust to be interred as my executors may think proper and my soul to the memory of one gracious Redeemer.

1. I lend to my beloved wife, Elizabeth, the houses and plantation whereupon I now live with the land purchased of Thomas Smith containing 236 acres more or less, also four Negroes, Viz: John and his wife Kiziah, Isaac and Lydia, my carriage and two horses — and an equal share with all my children of all the household and kitchen furniture and stock of all kinds, during her natural life and at her death I will and desire that all I've loaned her, may be equally divided amongst my four children, Anderson Childress, Susan Childress, Sally Childress, and John W. Childress, and them and their heirs forever.

2. I give and bequeath to my beloved son Anderson Childress my lot in Murfreesboro adjoining the public square on which the storehouse stands being part of Lot #_____, the balance of which is so owed to Kingsley, also $1,250 in money to enable him to pay up the residue of his stock in bank which lot and money I hereby give and bequeath to him my son, Anderson Childress, his heirs and assigns forever.

3. I bequeath to my beloved son, John W. Childress, $2,000 in money to him and his heirs forever.

4. All the rest and residue of my estate both real and personal I give and bequeath to four children, viz: Anderson Childress, Susan Childress, Sarah Childress, and John W. Childress, to them and their heirs forever, subject, however, to the following regulations:

I will and desire that all my estate may be kept together undivided under the direction and management of my executors to be hired out

21

or worked together as they may think proper for the support and maintenance of my beloved wife and children whilst they remain single or under the age of 21 years, and request that they will all live together as one family and be supported out of my estate and whenever one of my children shall marry or arrive at the age of 21 years then to withdraw their equal portions or one-fourth of my estate so kept together (always accepting the property loaned to my beloved wife, Elizabeth), and the residue to remain together for the use and benefit of the remainder.

5. I will and desire that my executors sell all my lands in Rutherford County in such lots as will in their opinion best suit purchasing (always reserving the tract of 226 acres loaned to my beloved wife and 80 acres adjoining thereto beginning on the bank of the river, by northwest boundary of the tracts I live on and running north for compliments) and all of my lots in the town of Murfreesboro not before divided and all or any part of my lands or lots (in the state of Alabama) and a good and lawful title to make to their purchase and whatever of my land they think proper to retain for the benefit of my children, desire they will pay up the several installments on them as they may become due.

6. I hereby nominate and appoint my friend Samuel P. Black and my son Anderson Childress executors of this my last will and testament. In testimony whereof I have hereinto set my hand and affixed my seal this tenth day of August, 1819.

Signed, Joel Childress (seal)

Signed and sealed in the presence of us — Joseph McMann, Blackmon Coleman, and Edmond Jones

Death must have seemed imminent at the time Joel Childress wrote this document. It was written August 10, 1819, and his death came on August 19, 1819. The will was of such detail and such clarity that he must indeed have been of sound mind.

Anderson Childress recorded and registered a detailed account of the personal items in the estate.[1] The slaves were entered by their first names, no family name given. Of 34 slaves, there were 5 men, 13 women, 7 boys, and 5 girls. The list of books left in the estate named 64 volumes in all, largely classical. This was probably a much larger library than that found in the ordinary home, even a wealthy one. The rest of the items were what would be found in the home of the affluent who aspired to be well educated.

The estate of Joel Childress left the family very comfortably situated. There is no mention that Susan or Sarah contemplated any return to Salem. They remained in Murfreesboro to console and aid their mother.

Sarah was well educated for her time, even though the last of her formal education came at the age of 15. There is no question that she was a very intelligent woman who made the best of her educational opportunities. However, some of her inadequacies are revealed when one reads letters written by her and addressed to her husband. A representative letter is addressed from Columbia, June 15, 1839:

> *Dear Husband, You did not leave me any direction where to write or direct anything to you. These letters contain information I thought might be useful to you, and I have thought proper to enclose them to Major Bill's with a request that he would send them to you. There is nothing occurred since you left of importance. I have only heard from you by General Pillow [Gideon J. Pillow] since you left. Why don't Knox [J. Knox Walker, Polk's nephew] write to somebody? I'm anxious to hear from you, not political prospects only but your good health. Affectionate wife, Sarah Polk*[2]

Sarah's lack of a superior education was compensated by her tact and charm. Much has been written about the appearance of Sarah Polk, and the various opinions about her beauty — or lack of it — differ greatly. The writers, perhaps to enhance the romantic element of their account, have referred to her as "beautiful" or "handsome."

"Mrs. Polk is a very handsome woman," said one English lady after visiting the White House. "Her hair is very black, and her dark eyes and complexion remind one of a Spanish donna."[3] About Sarah at age 16, it was said, "Sarah was already becoming a typical 'Spanish type' beauty with large brown eyes, and long dark hair framing her oval face."[4] And "Sarah Childress was not a beautiful girl, but she was considered something of a 'catch' largely because her family was wealthy and socially prominent."[5]

Sarah Agnes Wallace, writing about Sarah Polk, observed, "From various portraits of Sarah Polk by Healy and Brady one gets the impression that she was a strong rather large woman, cold and determined in purpose."[6] A biographer of her husband wrote, "Sarah had the potential for being quite an asset to James [Polk], for she was well educated, attractive, and self-assured."[7]

Perhaps in general such ladies are portrayed much as the writer perceives them or wishes the reader to perceive them. Probably nearer to the truth were these words written after Sarah's marriage to Polk. "Despite her plainness the curious neighbors found James' twenty-one-year-old bride an attractive girl."[8]

Sarah's portraits done by Healy and Brady showed that she had a distinctly aquiline nose. Her hair was long and dark, her eyes were large and dark, and her skin was dark. Perhaps the words "striking" or "handsome" were better suited to describe Sarah. One may venture to say that Sarah was handsome — beautiful, never.

The beginning and progression of the romance between James K. Polk and Sarah Childress is surrounded by much conjecture. One is led to think that the recorders of those real and supposed encounters have been tempted to inject an element of romance. They were first supposed to have met in Murfreesboro, Tennessee, by sheer accident at Bradley Academy, where she was, with her sister, being tutored after school by Samuel Black. The two were supposed to have been introduced by Anderson Childress, Sarah's brother. Sarah was nearly eight years younger than James. She was barely in her teens and he was a grown man at the time of the first encounter at Bradley School. It seems unlikely that any romantic fires were lit by that brief meeting.[9]

It was a reception in honor of Governor and Mrs. Carroll that the first well-documented meeting between Sarah and James occurred. The reception was attended by Felix Grundy, a former chief justice of the Supreme Court of Kentucky, and by General Andrew Jackson, an intimate friend of Grundy. James was said to have at first seen only Sarah's reflection in a mirror. "Across the crowded drawing room he saw for a moment the mirrored image of a slender girl with olive skin and soft brown hair. 'She's beautiful,' he thought, and started treading his way in her direction."[10]

Sarah was conversing with General Jackson, and James felt that Jackson would almost certainly introduce them, but by the time James reached them Sarah had gone. He made his way through the throng on the way to the library, where he found his old friend, Anderson Childress. They had conversed for a few moments about their days at the academy, and they were waiting at the foot of the stairs when Sarah reappeared and James recognized her as Anderson's younger sister. Anderson introduced them and asked Sarah if she remembered James, and she responded, "Why, of course I do." Anderson then offered James a ride in the Childress carriage, and as James sat beside Sarah, they became better acquainted.[11]

As Sarah looked at James, she saw that he was a little above average height, had a lean figure, and a broad forehead topped by a crop of brown hair.[12] Anderson asked James what had caused him to be in Murfreesboro, and James replied that he was chief clerk in the legislature and that he would be there until the end of the term, at which time he would return to his law practice in Columbia, Tennessee.[13]

One anecdote portrays Andrew Jackson as a heavy-handed matchmaker. Polk, nearing the age of 30, was discouraged because he felt that he had reached a dead end in his career with his work as clerk of the legislature. James asked Jackson what he should do to further his political aims. Jackson told him that he should settle down and become a sober married man. Polk in return asked the general just what lady he had in mind as a wife for him. Jackson replied, "The one who will never give you trouble. Her wealthy family, education, health, and appearance are all superior. You know her well."

"You mean Sarah Childress?" asked Polk, thoughtfully. Then after a brief pause he started off, saying, "I shall go at once and ask her."

Polk apparently had not thought of her as a marriage prospect. Now he thought of her as a means to an end.[14]

On her part, Sarah said at some time during her courtship that she would not marry him unless he ran for the legislature. In another version, James is supposed to have told her that he believed she would not have married him if he had remained a clerk of the legislature.[15] The story is repeated in many places that Sarah urged James to run for the state legislature, and when he ran, she agreed to marry him.[16] The courtship lasted for four years. For three years James's political activities kept him in Murfreesboro, and during that time he pursued Sarah persistently. He finally persuaded her to marry him and the time was set for an indefinite date the following year.[17] James did not wish to delay the marriage and tried to persuade Sarah to set an earlier date, but she insisted that such a wedding would require a lot of planning. In reply to his request she said, "I'm afraid not, Jim, I had to order dress material, some of it from France and England, and it takes several days just to make one gown. The seamstress is doing the best she can, but she will need several more weeks. She isn't just making a wedding gown, you know. There are other dresses and bonnets and sheets. Susan, Mother, and I are sewing pillowcases daily, and things just as fast as we can. You want your wife to be well dressed, don't you?"

"Yes, but not if it keeps her from becoming my wife," James replied.[18]

The clerk of court of Rutherford County issued the license authorizing the wedding of James Knox Polk and Sarah Childress on Thursday evening, January 1, 1824. The marriage rites were performed by the Reverend Henderson, pastor of the Presbyterian church.[19]

The ceremony was elegant. James and Sarah had protested that they wished a more simple affair, but Sarah's mother was determined that, befitting their station, it should be an elaborate event. There were eight attendants, who followed the bride and groom to an improvised altar in the parlor. The wedding supper was a bountiful seven-course meal. The guests were entertained by sentimental music provided by black musicians. The gala celebration lasted until midnight, when the candles were extinguished in the large chandeliers under which Sarah and James had received congratulations.[20]

Andrew Jackson, who had been invited, sent his regrets, but his adopted son, Andrew Jackson Donelson, was among the guests. The wedding celebration was planned to continue a full week with the newlyweds' friends participating in the festivities. The evening following the rites, Mr. R. Lytle gave them a party. The second day after the wedding, Susan and William feted them with a lavish dinner. They were compelled to refuse many other invitations, for they were due to be in Columbia, Tennessee, on January 8, and the roads were mired by torrents of rain, which made traveling very difficult. They did not wish to be late, because in Columbia, the Polk family was preparing a reception to honor the union. The young couple, for fear of bad traveling conditions, left two days earlier than they had anticipated. The road between Murfreesboro and Columbia was a quagmire. They had to stay overnight at a farmhouse to wait until the water level in the river fell to a fordable level. James and Sarah reached Columbia ahead of time, tired and muddy, but happy.[21]

To greet them at the family home were numerous Polks, including brothers John and Bill, and sisters Ophelia, and Naomi.[22] Maria and Elizabeth were apologetic for their husbands' absences, saying that they had not known when to expect the newlyweds. Fourteen-year-old Naomi delivered the welcome speech.[23] Sam Polk, James's father, gave the newlyweds, as a wedding gift, a horse, a cart, a water barrel, a young male slave, and a two-room house with slaves' quarters. Apparently there was no well at their new home, so water had to be hauled from their in-laws' home.[24]

In some accounts, it is claimed that James and Sarah lived in a rented house during their first year of marriage. After their first year they moved into a house of their own across the street from Sam and Jane Polk, James's parents. Their home had an unfinished second floor and a separate kitchen and smokehouse in the backyard.[25]

The Polk women, especially Jane, were strong Presbyterians, and Sarah had been raised by her mother to be a strict observer of that faith. Soon after the couple moved to Columbia, James bought a pew in the new Presbyterian church. Thereafter, when James was in town, he was a faithful attendee at church with Sarah.[26]

Sarah's Presbyterianism is, indeed, something that must be taken into account when we think of her and her possible influence on her husband and the politics of their time. Whether or not she absorbed a thorough infusion of Calvinism one cannot be sure, but there is much evidence that she did believe in predestination, which — among other things — may have affected her views on slavery.

James was absent a great deal on legal and political business, but Sarah was not lonesome, because the Polk clan provided her with more than ample company. She became very close to her mother-in-law, Jane Polk. James bought a carriage in which he and Sarah frequently made the 50 mile trip to Murfreesboro to visit Sarah's family. Due to heavy rains that occurred at times, the roads and streams were difficult to pass.[27]

During their first two years of marriage, Sarah saw very little of her politically ambitious husband. It is felt by many historians that his ambition was abetted by her own aspirations. James had a very distinguished record in the legislature, and there was much conjecture on his possibly being a candidate for the U. S. Congress. At the close of the 1823 session Lucius Polk let it be known that James was one of the first young men in Tennessee politics.[28]

After serving in the Tennessee House of Representatives from 1823 to 1825, Polk was elected by plurality over five candidates to the U.S. House of Representatives. When the time arrived for James to go to Washington, Sarah was eager to accompany him, but he felt it was better for her to remain at home. He explained that he did not wish to expose her to the hazards and discomforts of the trip. The route from Columbia to Washington was long, the accommodations were poor, and they would have to spend the nights in farmhouses along the way.[29] In the fall after taking office, James left Sarah in Columbia, despite her protests. Starting out on horseback to the nation's capital, he took a stagecoach for the last leg of the journey from Baltimore to Washington. Most of the legislators could not find decent housing in Washington and so left their wives behind. Maintaining a house in Washington was also more than most lawmakers were able to afford. So the legislators lodged in a hotel or inn and organized a mess with compatible colleagues.[30]

James's first letter from the capital convinced Sarah that he had been right to leave her in Tennessee. He wrote as follows:

> *Washington is like Columbia, the streets are dusty in the summer and muddy in the winter. Its public buildings are plainly constructed with wide gaps between them. The square before the Capitol is filled with huge stones and other building materials in readiness for its construction. The few inns and hotels are crowded and the prices are exorbitant. I am staying at Captain Benjamin Burch's boarding house on Capitol Hill, where I have a sleeping room and an office. I share meals with other congressmen. It is terribly lonely here without you, still I am glad I did not subject you to the hardships of the trip. However, this will be the last time I will be a Washington bachelor. Next year I will bring you with me, for I am going to make reservations for decent accommodations before this session is over.*[31]

To John Quincy Adams, Polk was lacking in wit, knowledge of literature, point of argument, grace of delivery, elegance of language, pathos, or anything else that could qualify him as an orator. However, Sarah was not seeking an orator. Mary Ormsbee Whitton, a biographer of Sarah Polk, wrote as follows: "Her James was a man who would stick to his party like a merchant to his business, and in due time industry and uprightness would be rewarded."[32] Polk hurried home after the spring session of Congress was over to foster his political fortunes back home and look after his business affairs.

By the end of the fall in 1826 the time came to return to the capital for the short term. Sarah was resolved that she would not be left behind this time. She had complained to General Jackson about her separation from James the previous winter. Now they traveled in their own comfortable carriage with two slaves, a maid, and a manservant. General Sam Houston joined them at Nashville, and at Knoxville Senator White joined the party. This lively group proceeded at an unhurried pace, spending their nights at inns and hospitable farmhouses.

Reaching Washington after their long journey, they resided a few days at Williamson's Hotel while they sought suitable living quarters. They finally found a residence on Pennsylvania Avenue, which they occupied with members from eight states.[33]

Some writers relate that during Polk's second term in Congress Sarah became pregnant. She is supposed to have lost the fetus before the doctor arrived. Dr. Roscoe, who arrived late, was supposed to have had trouble reassuring James that the mother would live. At that time Sarah was supposed to have told her husband that Dr. Roscoe had informed her that she could not have a baby.[34] At times, Polk's biographer, Noel Gerson — in order to add more dramatic effect — embellished the truth.

The truth, indeed, lay elsewhere. As a youth Polk was very frail and physically inadequate to farm or to go on surveying trips with his father. James's mother finally suggested that he be taken to see a doctor. James and his father made a 250-mile trip on horseback to see the regionally famous Dr. Ephraim McDowell in Danville, Kentucky.[35]

Dr. McDowell, who had studied medicine in Scotland, was brave enough to attempt surgery that no other doctor in the area dared do. By the time father and son arrived in Danville, James was sick and exhausted. McDowell insisted that his patient rest for weeks before he underwent surgery.[36]

Two well-written and popular Polk biographies, by Charles Sellers and by Martha Morrell, state that the surgery done by McDowell was the removal of gallstones, or cholecystectomy. However, this is not what happened. On October 20, 1856, approximately 40 years after Polk's surgery, Samuel Gross, professor of surgery at the University of Louisville, addressed the Kentucky State Medical Society. His description of the surgery done on James Polk did not mention the gallbladder. The actual surgery done, according to Dr. Gross, was a cystolithotomy (or a stone removal from the urinary bladder).[37]

In a letter written by John C. Wormsley in the fall of Polk's second year in Congress, there was some hint he wished that he and Sarah might have children. Wormsley wrote: "Bromlett has opened the campaign in high stile [sic] accept for yourself and Mrs. Polk my congratulation for the season with my sincere wishes that a residence at the city may prove felicitous in more ways than one."[38]

The claim that Polk had a cholecystectomy is refuted by records showing that the first cholecystectomy performed successfully in this country was done by Dr. John Dobbs in 1867, about 50 years after James's surgery.[39] We must relate here something about the procedure followed during the surgery performed by McDowell. Brandy was the anesthetic, how much brandy we do not know. James was held down by straps and some of McDowell's assistants. McDowell began his surgery with an incision through the perineum (the area between the penis in front and the anus behind). The opening was extended through the prostate and into the urinary bladder by means of a gorget, a sharp instrument designed for this purpose. The stones were located and removed by forceps. There were no complications of this surgery. However, there is well-founded speculation that Polk was made impotent by the surgery. This is based on the possible effects of the surgery done by Dr. McDowell's technique and by James being the only one of the seven married children of Sam and Jane Polk whose marriage was childless.[40]

Sarah was determined to do her best to further James's political career. Polk, in spite of his serious attention to matters of government, supported the social bent of Sarah. His approval stemmed at least partially from his belief that this would aid him politically. He appeared at dinners and receptions with Mrs. Polk, but was first and foremost concerned with the matters of state.[41]

Only a few decades earlier the incomparable Dolley Madison had made her brilliant husband popular. One difference between these remarkable ladies was that while Sarah was frugal, Dolley was a spendthrift.[42] In Dolley Madison's extreme attentiveness to her husband she was very solicitous of his welfare, but she did not seem to be greatly concerned with the affairs of state. In contrast, Sarah followed very closely the affairs of state and sometimes was able to advise her husband.[43]

At that time only a few officials with wealth could afford to keep big houses. The Polks adapted themselves well to the togetherness found in a boarding house. The parlor for common use of the group was limited to friends only. Soon, due largely to Sarah's conviviality, the Polks were admitted to the best congressional circles.

Eventually, Polk's farm interests in Tennessee became less profitable, so he began to raise cotton in Mississippi. "I am resolved to send my hands to the south," Polk wrote in September 1834. "I am determined to make some more money or lose more." The letter was concluded with a line asking Sarah to assist in ordering supplies for his new plantation: "Get Samuel Walker to buy them for me on the low-est terms he can." He ended the instructions with the following: "The Negroes have no idea that they are going to be sent to the south, and I do not wish them to know it, and therefore it would be best to say nothing about it at home, for it might be carried back to the Negroes."[44]

Although the attitude of Sarah and James toward their human property was not greatly inhuman, some of their statements such as the above reveal that they regarded slaves very much in the same way as they did steers and horses, which need not be consulted or have their feelings taken into account.

With the boarding house arrangement, the Polks were at various times closely associated with several congressmen, such as Hugh White of Tennessee, Leonard Jarvis from Maine, John C. Calhoun of South Carolina, and many others of note.[45]

Sarah was not just a politician's wife whose sole interest lay in entertaining. She was indeed involved so much in the parties, recep-tions, and balls that she was compelled to give up her piano lessons. Yet, beside the frenzied rounds of Washington society, she devoted much time to the complex world of politics. She was a knowledgeable woman who understood the principal political issues of her day. She also learned to a remarkable degree just how and where the lines of political power and maneuvering lay. This was not easy, because the political sands were always shifting. When James addressed the House, Sarah was in attendance, listening eagerly and critically to every word. In spite of her interest in James's career and the politics that surrounded it, she was careful not to let politics intrude in the drawing room.[46]

As soon as Congress adjourned in March 1827, Sarah and James returned home and found James's ailing father to be much worse. Dur-ing this respite from Washington, James went about the state mend-ing and strengthening political fences, but his concerns lay more with his critically ill father. Sarah devoted much of her time to her in-laws. She spent many hours reading to Samuel and trying to comfort Jane Polk. To compound their grief, Anderson, Sarah's older brother, was killed in a fall from a horse. Sarah, on receiving this news, left imme-diately for Murfreesboro. It was difficult to understand why a young man of 28 years and in perfect health should die so suddenly. When Sarah arrived at home, she was given the full details. Mary, Anderson's wife, related that he had gone hunting. Not taking his usual riding mare, he had elected to take a stallion that he had bought the week before. Mary said that about one hour after Anderson had left home, one of the slaves came running and yelling. The young lad explained that the stallion had returned to the stable, but Anderson was not on his horse. Mary sent some of the slaves to look for Anderson, and they found him by a fence. Mary, grief stricken and trying to regain some composure, said, "Oh, Sarah, his poor neck was broken."[47]

In November 1827, just as James and Sarah were preparing to return to Washington, his father died. James, the eldest son and co-executor of the estate, soon became the center of his family's disagreement on the provisions of his father's will. And to further add to the problem he had with his immediate family, he became involved in legal problems with Joel Childress's estate. Poor administration and inattention to business had squandered the once considerable fortune. All of this conflict became very bitter, especially in James's own family. Samuel was just buried when his married daughters and their husbands sued to break the will. They felt that the younger brothers and sisters had received more than their fair share.[48]

In the fall of 1827 James and Sarah returned to Washington by way of Kentucky and the Ohio River. They left their carriage at Lexington, Kentucky, and took a steamer over the Ohio to Wheeling, West Virginia. From there they went by stage to Washington. The roads through the Virginia mountains were rough and narrow. On this leg of the journey the carriage veered out of control on a sharp curve and overturned. Sarah was unhurt, but James received a scalp laceration.

Upon their return to Washington, James and Sarah were able to join a friendly and prestigious group in a mess. Those who met in the boarding house at Mrs. Anne Payton's were Senator White, John Calhoun, Senator Littleton Taswell of Virginia, Levi Woodberry of New Hampshire, Senator Malande Dickinson of New Jersey, Congressman William Haile of Mississippi, and Representative John Bills from Tennessee.[49]

In his second term in Congress, James became the eyes and ears of Andrew Jackson, who was a candidate for the presidency, and dutifully kept him informed on all congressional business. As soon as the session ended, May 1828, James and Sarah made their way home by stagecoach, taking time out to visit tracts of land inherited from James's father. That summer, riding horseback, Polk would campaign for Jackson all across Tennessee.

During the journey home, they had tried to cross a stream that was out of its banks from the heavy rain. As they started over the stream, a man on the far side yelled out to them to stop where they were or they would be drowned. James, who could not swim, stuck his head through the stagecoach window and yelled to the man on the bank that he would give him any amount of money to save Sarah. The man on the bank did not hear James, but Granfield Pillow, who was traveling with them, climbed out of the stage, swam to the shore, took the man's horse, mounted, and plunged back into the raging current. Sarah climbed out of the stage and onto the shoulders of the horse. Pillow took her to the bank without incident. She did not even get her feet wet.[50]

Chapter 3

In the fall of 1828, while James was campaigning actively for the election of Jackson to the presidency, Sarah developed a severe case of measles, and he spent a great deal of his time caring for her. After the election, when Jackson was assured of occupying the White House, the pro–Jackson forces were in an exultant mood, but Sarah had not yet recovered. She was reported to be looking pale and to have aged. Senator Levi Woodberry noted that "she looks as if she has grown 45 years older and seems distrait." However, the senator is not believed to have been a perceptive observer. Sarah was reported to have rebounded to a state of vitality and good spirits.[1]

In a letter of June 24, 1829, to his political agent William Rucker, James Polk expressed great concern that a case of smallpox had appeared about seven miles from Columbia. The patient was a man who had just returned from New Orleans. Polk's concern was justified because in that time the spread of smallpox in epidemic form could decimate a community. An urgent plea was sent to Nashville for vaccine and strong quarantine measures were taken. Every person in Columbia was to be vaccinated who had not been protected previously. There was also enough alarm to cause the officials of town to set up a hospital in the house of the man already afflicted. In James's concern for Sarah, he wrote that he expected her to go with a friend from Columbia to Murfreesboro in the next week.[2]

After James and Sarah had been back in Washington for a few weeks, they entertained several of their fellow Tennesseans at a dinner party. One of the guests was a Mr. Earle, an artist who was visiting President Jackson. Another guest urged James and Sarah to have their portraits done. Sarah's portrait, her first, pleased her husband. James exclaimed, "That is the picture of my bride. See those lovely raven curls clustering around her face, and look in those beautiful brown eyes. Mr. Earle had caught exactly the look of mischief that few people outside of myself ever see."

Polk supported President Jackson's opposition to the U.S. Bank and the unrestrained issue of paper currency, believing with Jackson that gold and silver should be the only negotiable currency. Polk put his belief into practice. He used the coins in trade and in the payment of his debts. Jackson's strong and unrelenting opposition to the U.S. Bank and every other bank was shared by many in Congress and was the subject of fierce debate.

Sarah shared most but not all of James's political views. On a journey to Washington, James and Sarah rested overnight, but the next morning, just as they were preparing to leave and all their luggage was closed, James looked into the room and said, "Sarah, get some money out of the trunk. I haven't enough money in my pocket to pay expenses during the day." Sarah, in a flurry, opened a trunk and began to rummage throughout its contents and found bags there of gold and silver currency.

"Don't you see how troublesome it is to carry gold and silver around? This is enough to show you how useful banks are," she said. To this James replied, "Sarah, you've turned your politics then, but all I want now is that money."[3]

Sarah and James were in the company of several congressmen and friends when James related this incident with some amusement and wit. A few members of the group traveling with the Polks who were not hard-money advocates were pleased that Sarah had joined forces with them.

Later, a gentleman who agreed with James on the monetary question came to call. Sarah remarked, "Mr. Polk, you and your friends certainly are mistaken about the bank question. Why if we must use gold and silver all the time, a lady can scarcely carry enough money with her."[4]

Sarah and James were separated during part of 1830 and 1831 while James was in Congress. That year, presumably in order to economize, she stayed at home. She soon was unhappy about their decision. James's letters home gave her some concern; he was lonely and overworked. Part of her concern arose from her husband's frail constitution. They never again allowed money concerns to separate them.[5]

James set out to Washington with some instructions. He was to have a handsome black dress made and sent home at the first opportunity. Sarah also ordered a spring dress of fashionable material that he was to bring with him, selected by Mrs. Overton. Sarah wrote: "If there is anything new or pretty in the bonnet way for the spring, you can get one, but leave that to the ladies." One gathers here that Sarah did not want to trust the selection of her headwear or hats to James. "If Mrs. Overton says there is anything new since I was there in the cape way, get one if it does not cost more than five dollars. Any little fashionable article of dress that does not cost much — buy one for me if it is entirely new and out of the way, that is if you think we have not got it here."

There is, however, a considerably different version as to why Sarah did not return to Washington with James that fall. She is said to have elected to stay at home to avoid further involvement with the heated Eaton affair.[6]

John Eaton, the secretary of war under Jackson, had married Peggy O'Neale, the excessively amiable daughter of a saloonkeeper. Cabinet wives and the wives of other notables refused to accept her socially. These ladies who had high-ranking husbands greatly resented the elevation of this lady of questionable repute into their own social circle and proceeded to vilify her. The reluctance of the wives of cabinet members to associate with Peggy angered Jackson so much that he asked for their husbands' resignations. A principal part of the scandal that surrounded Peggy was a story that John Eaton had been her lover and that she had been equally friendly with other men.[7]

Therefore, the winter of 1829 and 1830 had been a difficult one for James Polk. He was utterly loyal to President Jackson, but had a great dislike for Secretary of War Eaton. Sarah made this situation even more difficult by joining the barbed-tongued ladies of the capital in their battle against Peggy Eaton, referred to by the ladies as "Bellona," after the Roman goddess of war. It is a well-established fact that after Sarah took a stand she remained adamant in her opinion.[8]

Senator Levi Woodberry stated that only one member of Congress was henpecked more than James Polk. And now another colleague observed that Mrs. Polk "would sooner suffer Randolph's Black John to set at table with her than be on any familiarity with a lady [Peggy Eaton] whose only fault is the Secretary of War had made her honest instead of finding her ready made."

The Polks were very close to President Jackson, and Sarah seemed to sense that by staying at home she could avoid the bitter battle against the pretty wife of the secretary of war. Their stance in this affair did work for James's advancement. For the most part, Sarah retained her characteristic dignity and diplomacy where Mrs. Eaton was concerned. Encountering Peggy, she met her with a smile and a pleasant greeting. Mrs. Calhoun, wife of the vice president and the main instigator of this strife, was very critical of Sarah's avoidance of any ill will. Mrs. Calhoun actually accused Sarah of "social laxity," and scolded her about her failing to take a part in the crucifixion of "Bellona." One evening as Peggy Eaton was passing the White House, Mrs. Calhoun deliberately snubbed her as she passed in a carriage, but Sarah bowed and voiced a greeting.

"I don't see how you can speak to such a creature," Mrs. Calhoun said. "I think it is our duty to show we won't tolerate her in decent society." Sarah answered calmly, "No matter what I might think of Mrs. Eaton as a person I won't insult my country by any lack of courtesy to the wife of one of the highest officials."[9]

In January 1831 Sarah wrote to James that his brother Franklin had died of pneumonia. Later that spring Sarah learned that Marshall Polk, another brother, who lived in North Carolina with his wife and children, was also dead. Franklin had really died an alcoholic and pneumonia was the final catastrophe. Marshall had not done well in his law practice and left his estate heavily in debt. John Polk, another brother and a bachelor, died in September of the same year.[10]

Family woes and long hours took their toll on Polk. James wrote to Sarah on March 2, 1831, that Congress had sat until 4:00 A.M. He had become so fatigued that, for the first time, he was forced to go to his rooming house. He also wrote that he was low in spirits for he was fearing that he would be held so late in the House proceedings that he would be unable to catch the stage on time to go to Baltimore.[11]

Eventually, Sarah's exile from Washington came to an end. In a letter to John Coffey dated October 2, 1831, Polk wrote that Sarah would go with him to the capital for the winter term, and both he and Sarah would take pleasure in having Mary Coffey, John Coffey's daughter, as company on the way to Washington. Polk stated that the route and mode of travel would depend on the weather and the condition of the road. If the weather remained good, the Polks intended to go in their private carriage through North Carolina by way of Charlotte to see the widow and children of James's deceased brother Marshall. He wrote further that if there were any changes in plans, he would advise Coffey. Polk reported that Sarah was anxious to have Mary Coffey with them on the journey.[12]

In the spring of 1832 the country was involved in the Black Hawk War in Illinois, which was followed by an epidemic of Asiatic cholera that had spread from Quebec down the waterways into the United States. Sarah's mother wrote to her: "The cholera has hit Murfreesboro hard, all who can have fled to the mountains."[13]

Army troops shipped via the Great Lakes were severely afflicted; it was said that many units suffered more deaths from cholera than from the Indians. Of the people infected, over half died. The disease struck rapidly and killed in a short time.[14]

Cholera is bacterial in origin (bacillus vibrio cholerae); the infection is by the oral route. Drinking water may be contaminated by feces from a cholera patient. Flies and other insects are usually the carriers of the bacteria to food and drinking water.

There were to be other family problems besides the deaths of James's three brothers. His youngest sister Ophelia, married at 17 to Columbia physician John Hayes, had a Polk characteristic: hot-headedness. She created problems, not for herself alone, but for all of her relatives. James came to be the arbiter in settling some unhappy situations but — heavily occupied with his other personal business, his law practice, and his seat in the House — he naturally depended upon Sarah to help him attend to these family matters.[15]

By 1832 Polk's mother had only the youngest of her brood, Bill and Sam. James and Sarah took a great interest in the two young boys and became surrogate parents to them.[16]

Bill was first sent to the Bingham Preparatory School located in Hillsborough, North Carolina, and then to the University of North Carolina at Chapel Hill. He had in him that streak of wildness inherited by some of his brothers, and James had to call on Colonel William Polk, who lived near Chapel Hill, to help, asking him to "controll [sic] precisely as your own son" James's brother.[17]

After Bill had arrived at Chapel Hill, he began to create difficulties. He exceeded the amount of money allowed him, and his guardian had to state firmly how much he would be allowed to spend. Sarah, who shared all things with James, including his problems, was concerned about Bill's excesses. The younger brother Sam was of such disposition that he gave his mother Jane no trouble.[18] When Sam became 18, James intended to send his favorite brother to Yale. He accompanied the Polks on their return trip to Washington. They made an overnight stop at Whitfield, Virginia. Very early the following morning, James's body servant, Elias, came to the bedroom to light the fire. James asked what time it was, but Elias responded that he didn't know what time it was, but that "the sky is falling and Day of Judgment is come." James dressed hurriedly and went outside to view an astonishing spectacle. He could understand why the servant would believe the end of the world had arrived: hundreds of burning meteorites were lighting up the sky.[19]

James's duties in Congress were quite heavy and social activities were not permitted to infringe on them, but Sarah permitted no activity to interfere with churchgoing. If someone called on Sundays, Sarah, the Sabbatarian, was the one who greeted him. If one came to discuss matters of business with James, Sarah would, at church time, come into the parlor fully clad for church and would tell her husband that she had ordered their coach to pick them up. She would then politely invite the visitor to accompany them to church. They regularly attended the First Presbyterian Church, where Dr. Post was pastor.[20]

Polk and John Bell were rivals for the position of Speaker of the House. When the election was held, on the first ballot Polk was behind, and on subsequent ballots the Whigs drifted to Bell and the Jacksonians to Polk. Bell won on the tenth ballot and became the new leader in the Congress.[21]

On December 30, 1833, James delivered a powerful speech to Congress attacking the U.S. Bank. He spoke for the distribution of hard money to the state banks. President Jackson considered Polk his finest spokesman on this heated issue.[22]

As Congress drew to a close in June 1834, James was the hero of Democrats everywhere. He was toasted nationwide at July 4 holiday gatherings. But the long struggle in the House over the monetary policy had pushed James's already frail body to its limits, and he was forced to take to his bed for several weeks before Congress adjourned. Roger Taney wrote that "the labors you have passed through this session are enough to break down a man of iron."[23]

During 1834 John Bell and James Polk were engaged in a bitter political feud. The bitterness was largely on Bell's side. During Polk's early days in Congress, the Bells and the Polks had amicably occupied the same boarding house. However, Polk and Bell held opposing views of the bank and hard-money questions. In 1834 Polk and Felix Grundy had made plans to keep Bell from being reelected to Congress. They decided to persuade Governor William Carroll to run against him.

Much of the bitterness was carried on in the newspapers in Columbia and Nashville. Bell was ill fitted by temperament to stand the constant barrage of criticism leveled at him. Finally, Bell reached the explosion point in Murfreesboro, where he unleashed a diatribe of hatred against Polk in general and Jackson's policies in particular. Both factions were immediately aware that Bell had erred greatly.

The speech had not been reported fully in the Murfreesboro paper, and Polk, realizing that Bell had furnished him with real ammunition, insisted that the account be published in full. Sarah's brother, John Childress, and Dr. William Rucker set about getting the complete report published. Polk was advised that when he went to Murfreesboro to pick up Sarah he should make a speech, but he refused to do so. Friends of Polk, after several weeks, finally persuaded the newspapers to run the full story.[24]

In 1835 both Bell and Polk were reelected to Congress. After Congress recessed, President Jackson had remained in Washington because a fire had badly damaged the Hermitage. In addition, the old general had a political agenda that required his presence in the center of power. Jackson felt that he desperately needed Polk back in Congress and, furthermore, he wanted James to be Speaker of the House. On the first day of the new session of 1835 Polk was elected speaker on the first ballot. The bitter exchanges between Polk and Bell during the reelection campaign and the contest for the speakership sparked ill feelings that were to last many years. James's success in gaining the speakership was instrumental in making Martin Van Buren the next president. Bell soon began a systematic campaign to obstruct the operation of congressional business. Bell sought to embarrass and ridicule Polk. However, the speaker, at least on the surface, remained imperturbable.

When he imposed the "gag rule," Polk also became the verbal target of John Quincy Adams. As Speaker of the House, Polk mandated that all petitions relative to the abolition of slavery should automatically be referred to a select committee. The men appointed to the select committee were of such political persuasion as to assure the petition would never emerge from committee. Polk based his position regarding the admission of petitions on slavery on the presumption that the pleas were something that Congress had no constitutional right to act on.[25]

The Polks, as with most of the landed Southerners, were able to accommodate their views on slavery within their religious beliefs. It was as if somehow slavery was ordained by God. Much of James's income was invested in plantations, which were worked by slave labor. However, these slaves were valuable property who were not to be mistreated, and overseers who treated slaves too harshly were dismissed. The Polks in discussing their human property never used the word "slaves," but referred to them as "servants." This would seem to suggest that consciously or unconsciously there must have been a feeling of guilt attached. They never sold their "servants" except for disobedience, and tried to keep black families together.[26]

Samuel Loughlin of Nashville, Tennessee, in a letter of August 20, 1835, asked James to present his respects to Mrs. Polk and offer her his congratulations on being a member of the Congress elect.[27] One wonders if Loughlin was not impressed by the politically knowledgeable Sarah and her influence on the new speaker.

The topic of a letter from Sarah's brother, John Childress, from Murfreesboro, dated November 2, 1835, was political in nature. The local papers at that time were the main outlet for political opinion; the politicians and their followers fought to gain control of the newspapers, such as the *Columbia Democrat*, the *Columbia Observer*, or the *Nashville Banner*. John also stated that he wanted to see Sarah and James before they left for the capital. At this time James had become a force to be reckoned with as Speaker of the House.[28] William Polk, James's brother, wrote from Columbia, Tennessee, on December 21, 1835. Young William had just received the news that James had been elected to the speakership and wished to congratulate him. He also added his love to Sarah.[29]

After James rose to the speakership, he and Sarah moved into a suite of rooms on Pennsylvania Avenue. The move was taken because James in his elevated status was not permitted by protocol to live, as they had been, in a common mess. James explained to Sarah, "The principal reason for this is that awkward positions might ensue when the affairs and measures of Congress are discussed at meals." Sarah in a witty retort said, "As would inevitably happen, and if you were there they couldn't openly criticize the Speaker, could they?" James answered, "Hardly, neither do I want to be subject to a charge of overintimacy by a small group of congressmen to continue to share a house with them."[30]

Sarah remained in the capital for most of her husband's tenure as speaker. She said, "The Speaker, if the proper person and with the correct idea of his position, has even more power and influence upon legislation, and in directing the policy of parties than the President or any other public officer."[31] Everything we can learn about Sarah Polk indicates that she had more than adequate skills to enable her to help James's career in the political arena. Sarah was always aware of her need to conduct herself as befitted the wife of a congressman. She would not allow herself to become involved in any activity that was not suited to her position, or could lead to criticism of her husband.

The wife of a cabinet member once invited Sarah to the races. She wished Sarah to go because two prominent gentlemen from Tennessee were racing their horses, animals that had distinguished bloodlines. The lady even offered to pick up Sarah in her private carriage and take her to the racecourse. Sarah thanked the lady but politely declined to go. Later when Sarah and the lady met at a party, Sarah was asked, "Oh, why did you not go with me today?" Sarah replied that she refused because she had never gone to the races and did not wish to violate her rule.

The lady responded, "Well, that is a reflection on me." Sarah replied, "Oh, no, not at all. You are in the habit of going, I am not."[32]

James as speaker was under unrelenting stress. Day after day his opponents in Congress, including John Quincy Adams — who was a veritable thorn in his flesh — baited and assailed the speaker. Although on the surface James appeared calm and unflappable, underneath he was feeling the stress. He slept poorly, his food did not digest well, he lost weight, and he became weary. He was also plagued with repeated colds during that winter. These problems, added to his already frail constitution, were a cause of great concern. Sarah, always near, tried hard to protect James and she did relieve him of many onerous chores. However, there was no way she could keep him free from the intense, everyday pressures of his job. Sarah was concerned that he might have a major health problem. Both James and Sarah were eager for the end of the session so James could return to Tennessee for a period to recover.[33]

As Congress ended on March 3, 1837, Andrew Jackson was ending his political career with great reason for satisfaction. He had put an end to the U.S. Bank, which he hated, the federal debt was paid, and the rage for internal improvement was in check. The ill and worn old general had left office at the peak of his popularity. A. J. Donelson, Jackson's stepson, had to hurry home because of the illness of one of his children, and he asked the Polks to travel with Jackson on his return to the Hermitage. On their return to Tennessee the party traveled the first leg of their journey by the Baltimore and Frederick Railway. When their railway car became uncoupled, both Sarah and James escaped without injury. The party boarded a steamboat at Wheeling, West Virginia, and journeyed down the Ohio. Along the way there were many stops so that the returning president might be acclaimed. While traveling on the river, Jackson developed a cold and felt quite tired and ill. The party boarded another steamer at the mouth of the Cumberland and arrived safely at Nashville, where the Polks delivered the aged and ailing Jackson to Donelson.

Mid–1837 saw the country in the midst of a major depression, and elections in Tennessee returned only James Polk and two other Democrats to office.

The Polks seemingly were never free from family problems. The impetuous youngest brother Samuel was suspended from Yale for participating in a riot. After his expulsion he went to Washington to live with James and Sarah. But in June 1838 his academic problems were forgotten for at that time he developed full-blown symptoms of pulmonary tuberculosis.

Sarah and James, continuing their parental relationship to the family, took Sam to New York and then to Philadelphia to receive the best medical consultations available. The doctors held out no hope for Sam, and the Polks began their sad journey back to Columbia, Tennessee. James, already a frail person, was exhausted by the physical and emotional strain. He had done everything possible for his youngest brother. However, Sam was still alive when Sarah and James returned to Washington in the fall.

But family woes were not ended. Bill, the one who had caused Sarah and James the most problems, killed an attorney in a pistol duel on the streets of Columbia, Tennessee. The dispute arose because the attorney had called the young Polk a drunken fellow. Bill was, due to peculiar frontier justice, sentenced to six weeks in jail and a modest fine. Bill sent a message to Sarah that he could not forget her kindness, which had been "more the kindness of a mother than a sister."[34]

James's seventh and last session in Congress was one that was no less harassing than the others, for he was still in the company of the unrelenting gadfly, John Quincy Adams, and his old political enemy, John Bell of Tennessee. He feared that Bell might displace him as

speaker in the next session of Congress, and he felt that he had reached
a political dead end. These considerations were important in his decision to run for governor of Tennessee in the spring of 1839. James rode
horseback many hundreds of miles in his campaign for governor, and
in August 1839 he was elected by a majority of 2,462 votes.

The Polks bid a sad goodbye to their many friends in the capital.
Some had known and been good friends of the Polks since James had
come to Washington in 1825 as a young junior congressman.

Among the guests at the final reception were Mrs. William Seton
and Mrs. Joseph Gales, wives of the publishers of the *National Intelligence*. Speaking to Sarah, Mrs. Seton said, "I am very sorry that you
are going away. We have had many pleasant hours together, but while
I am sad on account of losing your society, there is a feeling of joy-
ousness connected with it which I will not keep from you. When Mr.
Polk is gone, he will not be electioneering against Mr. Seton and will
not record his vote against him."

Mrs. Seton was referring to James's use of his influence in the Congress to keep Seton and Gales from obtaining the contract for doing
the public printing. Sarah commented afterward, "She was a perfect
lady, and she would not have said that behind my back."[35]

During the campaign, Polk, who thought he had seen the last of
the spiteful John Bell when he left the House, was surprised to spot
his political enemy in the audience at Lebanon, Tennessee. He was
even more surprised after his debate with Governor Buchanan when
Bell asked to be allowed to say a few words. For over an hour Bell
vented his spleen, running the gamut of invective. According to Bell,
James Polk was without honesty, decency, or integrity. "James was a
pliant tool, trader, apostate, and Tory," he was a "liar ... hypocrite ...
a tyrant ... and a sycophant."[36]

When James was running for governor of Tennessee in 1839 Sarah
remained at home, but she worked equally hard for his election. She
actually coordinated his campaign. She arranged his schedule for speaking appearances, mailed out campaign literature, and handled his correspondence.[37]

On May 12, 1839, James wrote to Sarah from Dandridge, Tennessee:

> *My Dear Wife,*
> *Since I wrote you from Knoxville, I have addressed the peoples of
> Sevierville and Jefferson. Two of my weakest counties in the state. At*

the last election Cannon (Newton) received the majority of 10:1 in these counties. I had a respectable crowd at Sevierville and a decidedly favorable impression was made. At this place [Dandridge] yesterday the assemblage was not large and a death in the town prevented most from attending. In both counties there is a decided gain, and our strength is daily increasing. Carter was here on yesterday; he made a ranting demagogical speech but said nothing personally offensive. He intends, I am told, to follow me through his district. If he does and shall interfere with me, I shall have no difficulty in disposing of him. My information from Washington, Sullivan and Hawkins, is of the most favorable character; and I now think it is a reasonable calculation to say that I will receive a majority of the votes in east Tennessee. My health continues to be as good as usual but my horse has been taken so lame that I am compelled to leave him here. My friend General Anderson has been so kind as to lend me his, and will send mine to me on my return.

Tell my friends that I am somewhat fatigued but will be able to go through the campaign and that I am in high spirits at my prospects. From Greenville I will forward to you my appointments for the counties on the east side of Tennessee.[38]

Sarah's ability to charm the males who surrounded her is reflected in a farewell poem from one of her admirers, the brilliant jurist Joseph Story who, with Justice John Marshall, did much to clarify the powers that had been given to the Supreme Court by the Constitution. When James became Speaker of the House, he and Sarah had a suite of rooms in the Elliott Building, which also housed the Supreme Court. Sarah met frequently with the justices and their families. When the Polks left Washington, many members of the court expressed by letter their feelings of loss. No one was equal, however, to the staid Justice Story, who expressed his sadness in verse:

> To Mrs. Polk:
>   Lady, I heard with saddened heart
>   the melancholy strain:
>   so soon from these fair scenes depart
>   ne'er to return again.
>   How swift hath blown the busy hours,
>   since we as strangers met;
>   and some so bright, so strewed with flowers
>   are fresh in memory yet.
>   For I have listened to thy voice
>   and watched thy playful mind.

Truth in the noblest sense thy choice
yet gentle, graceful, kind.
Oh, may thy future days be blessed
with all our hearts approve;
The sunshine of a spotless heart
the joy of mutual love.
Farewell; and when thy distant home
cheered by thy smile shall be
To know the past thick fancies come,
I ask one thought of me.
Joseph D. Story
Washington, D.C.
February, 1839

The state capital of Tennessee had been moved from Murfreesboro to Nashville in 1827. But there was no governor's mansion, so James and Sarah rented a large dwelling on Jarrett Street, which was known as Grundy Hill.

On October 14, 1839, James Polk was formally inaugurated as governor of Tennessee. One newswriter, Harris, of the *Nashville Union*, noted the presence of General Jackson and that his health was apparently improved. Sarah was present with other members of the Polk and Childress clans. She, ever ambitious for her husband's career, thought that the governorship was a definite step upward.

The governor's message was felt to be a sound one. However, it was evident to his listeners that his interest remained national rather than local. His recommendations were duly considered by the legislature, but even the members of that body seemed to be more interested in daily practical politics for the national party than enacting laws for the good of the state.[39]

During the campaign, the Whigs had charged that Polk had only used the governorship as a stepping stone to achieve the nomination of vice presidency on the ticket with Van Buren. The charges seemed to have had some reasonable basis, for shortly after his inauguration the state senate began to consider nominating James for vice president.[40]

Whenever James was out campaigning, Sarah was always concerned about his physical condition, and her letters indicated that for a good part of the time she was not aware of where he was on his campaign trail. The Wednesday evening after the inauguration Sarah and

James received a large number of well-wishers at their new home in Nashville. James's mother, Jane, and Sarah were the only ladies present. Jane was interested in talking about the beautiful homes in Nashville. There was the McNairy place, where James and Sarah had attended a party honoring General Lafayette in 1825, and the Felix Grundy place, later to be Polk Place. These were stately mansions. They were also not far from the John Bell mansion. Jane remembered the animosity between Polk and Bell and did not mention the latter's home.[41] The conversation then settled on a discussion as to whether Murfreesboro would not have been the more suitable place for the state capital. James felt that Nashville's location made it the ideal place for a permanent capital but Sarah disagreed. She noted that Murfreesboro was closer to the exact center of the state and that, historically, it had as good a claim as Nashville to that honor. Polk continued by saying that the presence of the Cumberland River made Nashville more accessible to the rest of the country. He stated that the development of the steamboat had made all other means of transportation outdated. Sarah immediately countered, "But what about the steamcar?" Sarah, at this time, as she had in other instances, demonstrated that she had a clearer vision of the future than did James.

The state capital, Nashville, at the time James became governor, was a town of 6,929. Nashville could boast three newspapers: the *Republic Banner*, the *Nashville Whig*, and the *Nashville Union,* all of which were partisan in their views. These newspapers were carefully read for political opinion, so it was very important for a politician to have some control of the editorial content of a newspaper.

Nashville had a character of its own from its beginning. Sarah merged almost immediately into its social life. "Nashville has been a cake town since wheat flour became available, which was sometime around 1795. By the middle of the nineteenth century it was a cake town indeed."[42]

After the Polks arrived in Nashville, James had very little time for much social life. He became deeply absorbed in his new duties as governor and in addition was having financial difficulties. As a congressman, he had never had sufficient money to pay his expenses. Now the family was still in debt for their plantation, and a depression had reduced their income. A continued outlay of money for circulating pamphlets, traveling expenses, and expenses incurred in maintaining control of the *Nashville Union* had left Polk in debt. The governor's salary of $2,000 was far from adequate to pay their expenses. Compelled to borrow large sums of money, he still could not make ends meet. His financial condition was finally improved when his plantation became profitable enough for him to gradually pay off his debts.

Chapter 4

The governorship in Tennessee in 1839 was not nearly as complex or involved as the office of Speaker of the House. At that time the governor, holding the reins of state government, had a relatively simple job. The business of state was so routine that James could perform its tasks without secretarial assistance. There was, however, a great amount of official correspondence that had to be taken care of. Much of his correspondence — with which he was aided greatly by Sarah — was concerned with his role as party leader, and it was to this that James gave most of his time and efforts. That James aspired to some office more elevated than that of the governorship of Tennessee had long been apparent. In June 1840 he wrote to Martin Van Buren and suggested himself as a candidate for vice president on the ticket with Van Buren.[1]

In the spring of 1840 there were political stirrings in Tennessee. James was coming up for reelection as governor, and to oppose him was James Jones, a freshman legislator who was known better for his buffoonery than his statesmanship. Jones, like Happy Chandler, found that votes were more easily obtained by entertaining the common people than by debating the real issues. Jones was uneducated and totally without knowledge of government. However, he was intelligent, shrewd, and gifted in the art of clowning. Polk took seriously the affairs of state, but he was not equipped to debate with a clown who would not be drawn into a discussion of the issues. Jones was an entertainer.

Sarah, who remained at home during Polk's campaigning, continued to keep James informed on what was happening on the Tennessee political scene. There had been much to write about because in the spring and summer of 1840 consensus was building in Tennessee to present James as the candidate for the vice presidency.

On July 4, 1840, James announced that he would be a candidate for reelection as governor of Tennessee in 1841.

In a letter postmarked August 31, 1840, James's nephew, Samuel P. Walker, wrote about the political excitement in Columbia brought

49

about by the prospect of James becoming vice president. He added, "Tell Aunt Sally [Sarah] to come out. She need not be afraid and we will be very glad to see her, and I have no doubt that she will spend the time pleasantly."[2] (He was implying here that the danger of the cholera epidemic had passed.)

Sarah showed in her letters that she was James's eyes and ears for gathering all possible news related to the political scene. She gleaned all the gossip and hearsay on politics. She read and digested the contents of James's mail for his use and scanned all the newspapers for happenings in the world of politics.

Sarah wrote to James on December 30, 1840:

> Dear Husband,
> There's nothing happened of much importance since you left here. Appointment of Senator ——— so far as I have learned has been well received. Letters from Brown, John, and Ernie have come to you from Washington, written before Mr. Grundy's death, but anticipating the event preparing to make suggestion to you that it may be necessary and proper to call the legislature together for the purpose of electing senators, for it is almost reduced to a certainty that there will be a called session of Congress in the spring in which event Brown and Ernie write that you should be the person to be elected. I have given you their views written to you privately in as few words as I could express the intention. I do not understand matters sufficiently well to form an opinion. Yet, it does strike me that it is the right thing for you to do. They all seem to think that there will be a called session of the Congress early in the spring. Johnson [Cave Johnson] wrote that he would not run again and that it was necessary to have his successor settled and ready to take the field — this is the Washington news. As to home, there have come some letters from Memphis which seem to be of interest about the railroad directors and one from Mr. McLemore and one from George S. Gaines. There seems to be much feeling and excitement on the matter, but I suppose at Memphis you learn all about it. Here are some sheriff returns which is all that have come to hand. I saw Mr. Jerry George last evening but he does not seem to know much about anything. I have given Major such lessons as you have directed, all he seemed to know was the speculation about the new clinick [sic] all of which is to be seen in the papers now and before you left. Now as to myself, I have been waiting to receive the meat before I would leave for Murfreesboro. This is Monday and it has not yet come. I sent Elias to the man on Monday. He was not at home so you may see that I am in a state of uncertainty yet I will go on Saturday, I think, meat or no meat, though I do not

know that it will make a man think any more of his wife for her neglect of the domestic duties of the household. I will risk it at all events as directed. I will write again at Murfreesboro and hope to hear from you again soon.

Your affectionate wife, Sarah Polk[3]

Sarah wrote to James on Sunday, March 28, 1841:

> *Dear Husband,*
> *Fearing that you have left Murfreesboro before the mail got in this morning, I thought it best and safe to send a letter to Major Donelson to take to you. The proclamation came to hand last night and the officials from the department of state. I think you had better come part of the way tomorrow if you cannot come all the way. Your absence and the proclamation will or has been swallowed up in the prevailing topic of today—the March bank robbery—so you need not think that your absence will not make any difference. ... I look a little for you this evening but could not rest satisfied without sending a messenger to Major Donelson whom I knew was going to Lebanon tomorrow.*
> *Sarah J. Polk*[4]

On April 10, 1841, Sarah wrote to James from Nashville:

> *There is a calm here on politics and everything else. There is not much else said, only what appears in the papers. I do not think it likely that the Democrats will get any candidates in this county. There seems to be no prospect of doing so. I cannot gather much news as I see few persons. I have written all I know at present. You must write where to direct my letters to. I am not at all discouraged at anything I see in the papers or hear from any quarters, but when I think of the labor and fatigue you have to undergo I feel sad and melancholy and conclude that success is not worth the labor. ... If Jones does not frighten you home by the 15th you may tell him that your wife will be glad to see you.*[5]

In this letter Sarah expressed her great concern for her husband's well-being. We are led at times to feel that Sarah had an overwhelming ambition for her husband's political future, but her letter suggests that her solicitude for her husband exceeded her ambition. We feel that she is aware that James was encountering quite a bit of difficulty in his campaign against Jones and is trying her best to encourage him.

On April 10, 1841, James received another letter:

> *Dear Husband,*
> *I wrote to you that Jones' letter writers had appeared in the Banner*
> *representing you as used up by Jones, etc., etc. I do not believe anything*
> *that they put in the papers will have any effect so you need not be*
> *uneasy. I am not troubled at anything that has yet appeared.*[6]

Sarah was as usual, newsy. She was reading all the newspapers and reporting to James on the temper of the electorate.

James Jones, the comic running for governor against James Polk, was, contrary to some reports, trading anecdotes, jokes, and barbs with his opponent. Paul Bergeron states that anyone who believes that Polk was a dull and boring politician has never examined his gubernatorial campaigns, especially those of 1841 and 1843.[7]

Despite Polk's tremendous struggle — a struggle that left him exhausted — he was no match for the folksy campaign run by the Whigs and James Jones. Polk had never before suffered defeat as a politician, and the experience left him despondent. However, he immediately resolved to run again in 1843 for governor. For the first time in 24 years, James Polk was an unemployed politician. He had begun his political career in 1819 as clerk of the Tennessee State Senate. Shortly after his defeat James resumed his law practice in Columbia, and Sarah, while supporting James's political aspirations, was hoping that he might now lead a less stressful existence and that she and James could spend more of their time together. Her expectations came to an end when her husband almost immediately began to design his political strategy for 1843. He wished to run again for governor and use the office as the base to further his ambitions to become vice president. But the campaign of 1843 was a repeat of 1841, and James was again defeated by the waggish Jones.

James's second defeat in his run for the governorship of Tennessee seemed to have thrown his political aspirations into total eclipse for a time. An apparent period of profound depression drove him into seclusion. With his Calvinistic background, he had felt that one who was as hardworking and morally proper as he should not find himself losing an election. As usual, however, Sarah — his bulwark against misfortune — was at his side to encourage and convince him that his political career was far from over. As cheering as Sarah's words may have been, even she would have been amazed had she known what lay ahead.[8]

The prospect that Polk would soon be the new presidential nom-inee of the Democratic party could not be reconciled with common sense. Polk's arrival at such a height was, however, due to one man's miscalculation. As the time neared for the convention, Jackson was still supporting Van Buren for the nomination. Then two things occurred that led to Van Buren's failure to become the nominee. His first mis-take was to agree to delay the Democratic convention for six months, from November 1843 to May 1844. Had the convention come six months earlier, Van Buren would have almost surely have been the nominee. Up to that moment Van Buren was considered to be the choice of General Jackson for the next president. Jackson had been a strong espouser of the annexation of Texas. But Van Buren, as did Henry Clay, declared publicly that he was opposed to the annexation. This stand, taken only a few weeks before the convention, was his sec-ond great error. Van Buren had assumed his political strength was ade-quate without the support of Andrew Jackson.[9]

The former president's health was waning when he first heard of Van Buren's disaffection. Not believing what he heard, he required convinc-ing. Jackson sent word to James Polk, requesting a meeting at the Her-mitage.[10] This encounter with the old general marked the onset of Polk's campaign for the Democratic nomination for president. At the meeting Jackson stated strongly that the candidate should be an "annexation man" and reside in the southwest of the country as the boundaries were set at that time. Jackson declared that James Polk would be that man.[11]

When the Democratic convention met in Baltimore, there was a total of 266 votes. Had Van Buren been able to have the two-thirds rule revoked, he would have needed only 134 votes to become the nom-inee. For the two-thirds majority, he needed 177 votes. On the first ballot Van Buren received 146 votes: 31 short of what he needed. On ballot after ballot Van Buren not only failed to reach a two-thirds majority, there was a gradual diminishing of the number of votes cast for him. The convention then, under the leadership of Gideon Pillow, George Bancroft, and Benjamin Butler, began to promote the names of Silas Wright and James Polk as its candidates for president and vice president on the Democratic ticket.

While nothing was said to that effect, the first "smoke-filled room" may have been at that Baltimore convention. On the next day Polk was to be nominated on the ninth ballot. Wright, piqued over Van Buren's failure to be nominated, refused the second spot on the ticket.

Samuel Morse, using a grant from Congress of $30,000 to string a telephone from Baltimore to the Supreme Court room in the Capitol, tapped out the message, "What hath God wrought?" On May 29, 1844, he telegraphed the message from the Democratic National Convention that James K. Polk was the Democratic nominee to vie for the presidency of the United States. When the news of James's success was printed in a Washington newspaper, the people there, who expected Van Buren to be the nominee, did not believe what they heard.[12]

Polk was greatly surprised at this turn in his political journey. Before now he had set his immediate sights no higher than the vice presidency. He had had some thoughts of running for the presidency in 1848 or 1852, but never in 1844. Van Buren had been nominated eight years earlier under the rule that required two-thirds of the convention's vote to be nominated. Van Buren himself had been instrumental in getting the rule passed. He and his adherents had tried desperately to change it, but failed after a heated debate.[13] Now great plans for the campaign of 1845 were made at the Hermitage under Jackson's guiding eye.

There was an interval of five months between Polk's nomination and his election. Soon after James's nomination, Sarah began to help his campaign. This work was carried on largely from their home in Columbia, Tennessee. The arduous task was pursued all day long and late into the night. Both James and Sarah studied and filed correspondence related to the campaign. There were countless letters to be written to campaign workers and party leaders. Also, the newspapers had to be kept informed about James's stand on the issues, mainly the question of Texas annexation. There could be no doubt that James and Sarah worked as a team. It seems likely that James, with his frail constitution, would have broken under the strain had not Sarah been working at his side. They were undoubtedly extremely weary at times, but they doggedly continued until James was elected.

From what can be learned, it seems clear that Sarah was a most politically astute woman for her time. Extremely well versed in all the issues facing James and the nation during his administration, his wife was confident that he was equipped to confront and solve those weighty problems.[14] Sarah is acknowledged to have been a serious and very knowledgeable student of politics. She was also driven by an ambition that was almost boundless.[15]

Following the Democratic Convention, James arrived back in Columbia, where he soon received a summons from the Hermitage. General Jackson, on his deathbed, still wielded his political power. Hemorrhaging from his lungs and gasping for breath, Jackson expressed his view that Texas and Oregon belonged to the United States. Then Jackson said, "They are both ours and we are going to keep them."[16]

The conference at the Hermitage also covered the possibility of war with Mexico should the United States annex Texas. The old general felt that the Mexicans were only bluffing, but he added that the United States should wait until Mexico struck the first blow and then fight to win the war.[17] One suspects that the wily ex-president really meant that the United States should provoke Mexico into striking the first blow.

The election was very close. Polk won the plurality, not a majority, of the popular vote. Polk failed by 300 votes to carry his own state of Tennessee. He carried 15 states with majorities in all but Michigan and New York where he received a plurality. The total national vote was 2.7 million. Polk received 1,337,000, Clay 1,299,000, and in the electoral college vote Polk received 170 and Clay 105 votes. Polk's election to the presidency in late 1844 was the first time in U.S. annals that a dark horse had been elected to the presidency. When Polk had received the nomination on the Democratic ticket, people outside of Tennessee and the South had asked, "Who is this man Polk?" In Tennessee, where Polk had been in politics for many years, he was recognized to be a fighter, but the majority did not feel that his chances of victory over Henry Clay were great. Sarah, however, never seemed to be in doubt concerning the outcome.[18]

After the election Sarah and James visited Nashville and were honored at a reception attended by both Democrats and Whigs. Later that evening many buildings were illuminated in honor of the Polks.

In Columbia a sharp-tongued lady remarked to Sarah's niece Ophelia that she had hoped Clay would be elected because his wife was a good housekeeper and made fine butter. The two ladies exchanged a few strong comments on this matter. Ophelia related the exchange to Sarah who replied, "Now, Ophelia, you should go back to your friend tomorrow and tell her that you are sorry for the sharp replies you made. Also tell her that I said if I should be fortunate enough to reach the White House, I expected to live on $25,000 per year, and I will neither keep house nor make butter. This answer will not offend her, and neither will I be offended."[19]

James had spent a great deal of money running his campaign and he was heavily in debt. However, neither James nor Sarah was depressed by their financial problems. Both had demonstrated in the past that they knew how to live frugally. James wrote to Cave Johnson, a friend from Tennessee, and asked him to get rooms for Sarah and himself at Coleman's Hotel and to make sure that the rates were reasonable. They expected to arrive in Washington on February 20 and stay at the hotel until inauguration day.[20]

James and Sarah left Columbia by carriage, accompanied by two nephews, Marshall Polk — who was going east to college — and Knox Walker — who was to become James's private secretary. They spent the first night at Franklin, Tennessee, and arrived Wednesday at the Franklin Inn. That evening they were the guests of honor at an elaborate dinner and ball. The following night James and Sarah were guests at the Hermitage. James discussed many matters with the old general and sought his advice on the choice of his cabinet.[21]

After the celebration in Nashville, the Polks boarded the *China*, bound for the nation's capital by the Ohio River. On board were many friends and relatives who expected to attend James's inauguration. But their festive mood ended on the way, when the *China* ran into a storm that drove it ashore. There were no injuries and James and Sarah remained in their cabins, where the president-elect, unperturbed, sat and worked on his inaugural speech.

A preview of the Sabbatarian bent of the new first lady occurred on Sunday when a band of musicians came aboard to honor the Polks by playing throughout the day. Sarah deemed it improper for the band to play on Sunday and requested Colonel Vernon Stevenson, a friend of the family, to convey her wishes that the band should not play.

At every stop in Ohio and Indiana, Polk admirers crowded on board to see and welcome the new president and his first lady. From Wheeling, West Virginia, they went by carriage over the National Road to Cumberland, Maryland, and continued by train. The party was joined at a station near Baltimore by committees from Washington and Baltimore and the vice president elect, George M. Dallas, whom Sarah described as "a tall, elegant man, exceedingly handsome, and gentle."[22]

Inauguration Day dawned with a threat of war with Mexico. During the waning months of Tyler's administration, Congress had passed a resolution calling for the annexation of Texas. Tyler signed the House resolution on March 1, 1845, three days before Polk's inauguration.[23]

The day was overcast, rainy, and dismal, but the town was full of happy, brightly clad people. As was customary, the president-elect and the retiring president rode in an open carriage drawn by four horses and escorted by the chief marshal and his aide, who carried emblems of the new head of the republic: batons of hickory, decked with a profusion of ribbons. Polk and his attendants were received in the Senate chamber by the assembled Congress.[24] Sarah and her close friends and relatives viewed the ceremony from the Senate gallery.[25]

Sarah's spirits had not been depressed by the dismal weather as she dressed for the ceremonies. She had chosen a striped satin gown in wine red and silvery gray, with a V-neckline and long, closely fitted sleeves. Her thin waistline accentuated her lithe figure. Over this she wore a mantle made of lightweight, sand-colored wool, lined with a quilted rose taffeta. Her velvet bonnet matched the wine red of her dress. She adjusted her hat, pulled on her white lace mitts, and picked up what she referred to as her national fan, which had been presented to her. In the folds above a beautiful open-work ivory handle were 11 circles enclosing the portraits of the 11 presidents, from Washington to Polk. Each was inscribed with the name and the date of their terms of office. Above James's name was written "president-elect." In the flower-gilded spaces between these circles were illustrated the U.S. escutcheon and the statue of the goddess of liberty. On the reverse side was an oval picture of the signing of the Declaration of Independence.[26]

In a short ceremony Dallas was sworn in as vice president. The party then made its way to a platform on the eastern steps of the Capitol, looking down on what appeared to be a huge assemblage of umbrellas below. There, James Polk delivered his inaugural address.[27]

In Polk's speech he declared his belief in freedom of opinion, separation of church and state, and equality of all citizens. He praised the U.S. Constitution and the Union. He insisted he was neither a nullifier nor a latitudinarian. He vowed the strictest economy and a plain and frugal government. He pledged he would not be the president of a part only but of the whole people of the United States.[28] He also warned of the possible danger connected with an adjudication of the slavery question. He was happy over the expectation that Texas would soon be a part of the Union. The president also spoke of his confidence in his belief that the U.S. claim to the entire Oregon territory was "clear and unquestionable." He reechoed the old Jacksonian antagonism against the reestablishment of a national bank.[29]

Chief Justice Roger Taney administered the oath of office. When the ceremonies were over, the new president was greeted with shouts and cheers from the great crowd. The throngs present at the inauguration joined the procession and attended the new president to the door of the White House.[30]

The Bible upon which the oath was taken was a small one, printed in clear minion type and bound in black morocco. It was presented to Mrs. Polk by Alexander Hunter, chief marshal of the District of Columbia. On the flyleaf he wrote as follows:

> Madame,
> I feel it an honor and a duty to present you the sacred volume on which the oath of office of President of the United States was administered to your honored husband on the fourth day of March just past. I will not permit myself to doubt that it will be esteemed and preserved by you as a sacred and not unbefitting memorial of an event of interest to your family. It is calculated to unite in solemn association the recollection of the highest honor on this earth, with the bright hopes and glorious promises of another and happier sphere of existence. United with your distinguished husband and in the enjoinment of the utmost favor of his country and the highest station which their votes and their confidence can bestow, when time shall have passed and the troubles and the honors of this life shall have known their termination, may your union still continue undisturbed and blessed with that happiness which that Holy Book teaches, as the hope and the promise.[31]

It is astonishing how many men seemed to be attracted to Sarah and wrote to her and about her in high sounding prose and poetry.

On inauguration day hundreds of friends and office seekers invaded the White House. Polk was compelled to tell them over and over again that applications would be reviewed if properly submitted. After this fatiguing line of White House visitors had departed, James and Sarah dined quietly in their new official home with a few friends and relatives.[32]

The inaugural ball was held at Carusis Hall. In order to prevent the place being overrun by those anxious to see the new chief executive, there was an admission charge of $10. When the president and first lady entered and were seated, the dancing came to a halt, and the band played "Hail to the Chief," followed by a general reception.

Sarah recalled in later years that she wore a marine blue velvet dress, with a deeply fringed cape. When the ceremonies of introduction and handshaking were over, the Polks and their friends left the hall.[33]

Thus began the administration of James Polk. His wife was perhaps better versed in the game of politics than any first lady at any time, but she never made herself offensive by a display of this attribute. She did express strong opinions in her drawing-room conversation, but she was careful to say that "Mr. Polk thinks so." It is clear, however, that in their private lives Sarah was free in the expression of her thoughts in the field of politics, passing her own opinions on to James. She thought it important to digest all possible information available in letters and newspapers so that she could help him keep fully informed. Sarah became Polk's private secretary and is the only first lady to fill that position in the White House. She was in full charge of all White House papers, and if James was in need of any material long since filed, he could depend on Sarah to find it.[34] Sarah used her intelligence in an unobtrusive way: she was the power behind the throne.

Sarah read and passed judgment on all of James's speeches. He discussed freely the ever-mounting political problems with her, and even had her evaluate the cabinet's deliberations and decisions. In addition to being James's full-time companion and adviser, Sarah took time to hold two receptions each week and give a state dinner.[35]

James did not like to take time from his work to receive visitors so Sarah became successful in making friends for them both. She met every Saturday with the congressmen and senators. It became known among the politicians that Sarah was extremely well versed in national affairs. She listened and absorbed information that might be useful to her husband. Later in the privacy of their quarters they would discuss what she had gleaned from her conversations. Sarah had a mind of her own. There were occasions when James's cabinet had views that were opposed to his, and Sarah would agree with the cabinet. There were times when she could not change her husband's mind. In spite of their occasional differences in opinion, Sarah was always consulted.[36]

Sarah's preference to join the gentlemen in their discussion of politics and weighty affairs led some of her female guests to complain that she would never stay in the sitting room with them, but chose the company of the president and the male guests. Franklin Pierce, later elected president, said that he preferred to talk politics with Sarah over anyone else, including President Polk himself.[37]

Although Sarah tried to make it known that her husband's ideas and policies were his own, there seems no doubt that privately she exercised much more influence on his thinking than anyone else. One of James's political opponents commented that James Polk was one of the most henpecked men he had ever known.[38] Such, however, is far from accurate. Sarah and James had a deep and abiding mutual respect. She was devoted, supportive, helpful, and capable of giving good advice, but never domineering. James saw in Sarah a penetrating intellect: a woman whose advice was worth taking. He was physically frail, and had his wife been capable only of playing the role of White House hostess, his administration would have been far less effective and he might not have survived four years in the excessively demanding role of president.

It was felt that George Dallas, the vice-president who rarely got the president's ear, was jealous of Sarah's influence. Soon after James's inauguration, Dallas said of Sarah, "She is certainly master of herself, and I suspect of somebody else also."[39] Sarah did not regard it as unusual that she both shared her husband's interest in political issues and kept her ladylike manners. That Sarah's personal views of state affairs were rarely expressed openly may be credited to the fact that ladies of the early and middle 1800s remained meekly on the sidelines and never differed openly with their husbands. To keep her husband in the limelight, she gave him the credit for everything.[40]

The Polks had clearly defined scruples concerning what was and what was not proper for the first couple of the land. Soon after they moved to the White House, a gentleman sent a fine horse to the White House stable. When Polk became aware of the gift, he instructed his secretary to send the horse to a livery stable and to let the owner know where to find it. He would accept books, canes, and other items of small value, but refused expensive gifts. Later, Polk refused the offer of a carriage and horses that the citizens of New York wished to give him.

Sarah came under the same temptations. There was a naval officer who would tell the first lady about some rare articles he had seen in a far country and that he had wished to bring home and present to her, but he was aware of her reluctance to accept such gifts.[41]

When the Polks moved into the White House, they found it in a sad state of disrepair. The chairs had been reupholstered only once since the Monroes' occupancy and were in a terrible state. Congress, which had not worked in harmony with Tyler, had shown its displeasure in part by failing to appropriate money for refurbishing a sadly neglected White House. However, soon after the Polks took up residence in the mansion, Congress appropriated a generous sum for that purpose. The frugal president, however, declared his intention to use no more than half of the allotted money. During the very hot summer, the Polks found they could not endure the terrible smells of white lead and oil cloth from the repainting that was being done in their residence and were compelled first to move into a hotel and then into a private residence.

The White House was painted both inside and out, new carpets were put down, and new red velvet curtains were hung. A report stated: "The whole was in a Republican style — neat and sufficiently rich, without any indication of extravagance." At the same time Sarah was at work planning for the social season, training her staff of 15 servants, and purchasing more than $600 worth of gowns, which had been selected by friends in Paris.[42]

Sarah, when she entered the White House in 1845, left the management much as it had been in James Madison's time. The staff, of necessity, became larger because entertaining had increased greatly. This proved to be a physical and financial drain on the Polks. During the Mexican War, dinners and receptions were held continually.

Sarah was so concerned about the costs that even before she entered the White House she investigated the possibility of renting a house and using the White House solely as an office. When she finally moved in, she instituted cost-reducing measures. The main change was made in the number of staff who were on salary, replacing them with the Polks' own slaves, a strategy employed by earlier Southern presidents. Terminating the service of ten hired servants, she substituted slaves from James's homeplace in Tennessee and others purchased from his family and friends. To accommodate them, Sarah had some remodeling done in the servants' quarters in the basement.[43]

Mrs. W. M. Morrisey, wife of the secretary of war, was Sarah's favorite among the cabinet wives. She and Sarah frequently attended the Presbyterian church together. Mrs. Morrisey was a Baptist, so at times Sarah went with her to the Baptist church. During Sarah's 14-year stay in Washington while James was in Congress, she had been a faithful attendee at the First Presbyterian Church, which was located not far from the Capitol. When she returned as first lady, it was thought that she would worship at the Reverend Mr. Lowrie's church, not far from the White House, but she continued to attend her former church, which was considerably farther away. "I love the familiar place," she said, "and why should I not go there when it was my intention to ride, and a mile more would make no difference?"[44]

Sarah was a Sabbatarian. She kept her husband from conducting state business on Sunday. She even turned away a high-ranking Austrian official who came to present his credentials on the Sabbath. James, even though he was a Methodist by persuasion and refused to be converted to Calvinism, attended the Presbyterian church with his wife. Sarah was described as one who, with James in tow, came stylishly late and made a conspicuous entrance. On one occasion she was dressed covered from the neck down in a floor-length coat of heavy black silk moire and an angled, wide-brimmed hat, also black, crossed diagonally with a large white ostrich plume.[45]

The religious press was ecstatic. The *National Union* sang Sarah's praises with a veiled attack on the previous first lady, Mrs. Tyler, who had presided over a much more relaxed White House. "The example of Mrs. Polk's can hardly fail exerting a salutary influence. Especially does it rebuke the conduct of those ladies who professing godliness dishonor its profession by eager participation in the follies and amusements of this world."[46]

Chapter 5

There is some evidence that the domestic affairs of the president's house were not rigidly ordered by the first lady. On one occasion Colonel Thomas Hart Benton received an invitation to dine at the White House. When 6:00 P.M., the appointed hour, had come and gone, he asked, "Mrs. Polk, did you not invite us to come and dine at a certain hour?"

Sarah responded, "Have you not lived in Washington long enough to know that the cooks fix the hour for dinner?"

"Madame," he replied, "you have the advantage of me."[1]

Some individual who attended a White House party and left with the feeling that he did not have a good time observed: "Such introducing, such scraping, such curtseying, such jabbering of foreign compliments and violent efforts of some people to do the polite in uncouth tongue, such a clamor of conversation rages. The band, too, has become tiresome and the room is oppressively warm when the President enters the room leading a lady — probably Mrs. Madison, and followed by Mrs. Polk and all the great people of Washington."[2]

Sarah's weakness, if she had such, was her lack of interest in household minutiae. She rarely interfered in or directed the details of the White House dinners. Once a guest remarked that there were no napkins on the table; the first lady had not even noticed. The only thing to which she paid attention at her parties was the conversation. Often she would get so animated that she forgot to eat.[3]

It was necessary for Sarah to have a female friend outside family and political circles. She found such a friend in the person of Dolley Madison. It is perhaps not strange, if one has any understanding of human nature, that Sarah and Dolley sought each other's company: they were truly opposites. Both were devoted wives to frail husbands. But Dolley was not serious-minded like Sarah, and politics was her least concern. Dolley loved parties and fine clothes. She wore colorful gowns, elegant shoes, presided over elegant dinner parties, attended

balls, and played cards. "Mrs. Madison is as sprightly a dancing partner as I have ever had," exclaimed President Washington, after a party
in the spring of 1795.[4]

In late 1845 the Polks invited Dolley to a reception at the White
House. Dolley had become good friends with the Polks when she
returned to Washington to live permanently. She had an inclination to
associate with people who were younger than she. Sarah enjoyed taking the ex-president's wife on rides on pleasant afternoons, and Dolley was invited to every cabinet dinner and to all of the social func-
tions at the White House. President Polk always escorted her to the
table. The elderly Dolley was always dressed in black silk or velvet with
a kerchief of mauve muslin and lace around her neck and shoulders
and folded across her bosom.[5] Dolley was credited with humanizing
Sarah and James by the down-to-earth, kindly atmosphere with which
she surrounded herself. She was a waltz-loving, card-playing old woman
who dipped snuff.

Senator Rob Preston noted in his journal two years before her
death: "I was at a whist party with Dolley when Mrs. John Quincy
Adams was her partner and Lord Ashburton mine. Each of the three
was over 70 years of age." The truth was that all were near 80, but
Dolley kept up her lively spirits and social prestige in spite of a both-
ersome eye affliction and a son's extravagance that reduced her to
poverty. She was in such dire straits financially that she had to pawn
her silver.[6]

Sarah's taste in her personal possessions are evident in the clothes
and jewelry she wore. Her ball gowns are supposed to have been
designed and tailored in Paris; however, those dresses that have been
preserved have no label. Some of her apparel was made under her supervision by a seamstress and maid, Teresa, a free black woman. Her gowns
were elegant affairs, made of satin, grosgrain silk, or cotton mull. Her
skirts were long and full, or with deep flounces or trains. Some of her
most elegant outfits were topped by headdresses with sprays of ostrich
plumes, or turbans, like Dolley Madison's.[7] Her jewelry collection shone
with precious gems and cut and polished rocks and minerals. She had
mosaic necklaces and bracelets, white sapphire broaches, coral, and
ropes and jet and brilliance. Usually Sarah wore a cameo bearing the
president's profile.[8]

There are certain events recorded about the life of Sarah Childress
Polk that give us some true insight into the nature of this complex

woman. On one hot summer day Sarah, who was working with James in his study, put away her pen and walked over to a window. She looked out for a few minutes and observed some young blacks sweating profusely as they worked in the garden below. Then Sarah turned away from the window and addressed James: "Mr. President," she said, "the writers of the Declaration of Independence were mistaken when they affirmed that all men are created equal."

"Oh, oh, Sarah," cried Polk, looking up from his desk, "that is one of your foolish fancies."

"But, Mr. President," persisted Mrs. Polk, "let me illustrate what I mean." Sarah pulled him over to the window. "There are those men toiling in the heat of the sun," she said, "while you are writing, and I am sitting here fanning myself, in this house as airy and delightful as a palace, surrounded with every comfort. Those men did not choose such a lot in life, neither did we ask for ours; we are created for these places."[9]

From this vantage one is able to have great insight into the beliefs, not only of Sarah but also thousands of others of her time. Her Calvinism led her to believe that we are predestined to assume our various roles in society. It also became much clearer why Sarah and Bishop Leonidas Polk were able, through their Calvinistic beliefs, to justify the owning of slaves. Bishop Polk was a cousin of James Polk and was educated at West Point, but he resigned his commission six months after graduation to enter Virginia Theological Seminary. In 1831 he took orders in the Protestant Episcopal church, and in 1838 he became missionary bishop of the southwest. In 1841 Polk was consecrated bishop of Louisiana. He was one of the significant founders of the University of the South at Sewanee, Tennessee. At the onset of the Civil War he was commissioned major general in the Confederate Army. The reason for his assuming such high rank was based not on his military training but on the high esteem in which he was held throughout the South. His final rank was that of lieutenant general. General Polk had a large plantation and owned many slaves. He held the opinion, as did Sarah, that the state of slavery was preordained for some, and he was able to reconcile his religious beliefs with the owning of slaves.[10]

Some of Sarah's less desirable traits did surface from time to time and she could be very vindictive, especially when her husband had been criticized. John Van Buren, son of former President Martin Van Buren, was subjected to her displeasure after he had been critical of Polk's administration. John's unhappiness with the administration arose principally from his feeling that Polk had been the main cause of his father's failure to be elected to a second term. After Polk was elected president, John came to Washington and was highly critical of Polk's selection of recipients of patronage.[11]

In Polk's diary of November 1845 he wrote that John Van Buren had expressed the belief that Polk was bestowing the patronage and administering the government to ensure his candidacy for a second term.[12]

The younger Van Buren called several times on President Polk, but failed to pay homage to Sarah. Every time the president invited Van Buren to dinner, Sarah removed his name from the guest list. When once her husband, in a motion of goodwill, had invited him yet again, the ever-vigilant Sarah discovered the invitation before it was sent and burned it.[13]

James received a letter from Samuel Loughlin dated May 30, 1835, from Nashville, Tennessee: "I am glad a certain lady is in good spirits, and engaged in the amusement of politics, though from my heart I could wish she had some more amusement to amuse herself with, something more domestic, for instance. Wishing her forever happiness and her husband success, Samuel H. Loughlin." Samuel was a newspaper editor and a strong supporter of Jackson. He was, however, one who overindulged in drink and therefore was unreliable.

Loughlin was implying that he would prefer to relegate the ladies to domesticity. He could not believe that Sarah's interest in politics could amount to anything more than a diversion. He sorely misjudged the depth and seriousness of her interest.[14]

The truth is that Sarah was the first presidential wife to serve as her husband's secretary, and she did so without pay. She worked long hours beside her husband late into the night.[15]

She viewed her work as seriously as she did her religion. Both she and Polk would have been labeled today as workaholics. She was not known to expend her time frivolously. If they were compelled to spend more time than they liked entertaining, it was their custom to extend their work into the late hours when they should have been sleeping. James Polk was among the hardest working presidents and Sarah worked just as diligently at his side. It was Sarah's constant fear that his overworking, combined with his frail constitution, was endangering his health.[16]

Generally, first ladies did serve to act as hostesses and were not engaged in politics, but there have been presidents' wives who have been given credit for being advisers to their husbands. Helen Taft is said to have had an overweening, jealous appetite for power. It could not be said that Taft truly sought her advice. "Nellie," as she was called, was very aggressive in putting herself forward. She issued disclaimers about her influence, but her actions spoke much louder than her words. She ignored the protocol that said that the president should enter the East Room first. She charged ahead of Will Taft and greeted several guests while he was still working on his first couple.[17]

Woodrow Wilson also had an assertive, aggressive first lady whose influence did not come into play until Wilson became an invalid following his stroke in 1919. At the Peace Conference of 1919 in Paris, Wilson worked a long, exhaustive schedule, handling even the most unimportant details of the negotiations himself, without consultation. Working without adequate staff, he toiled for hours alone, working out the details of the Allied proposal and then typing out the response himself.[18]

Wilson trusted no one, not even his closest adviser. He even typed his own reports, fearful that there would be a leak. Wilson had, like Polk, a suspicious, distrustful attitude toward all others, even his closest friends. He could well be described as having a paranoid personality.

When her husband was totally disabled, Edith Galt Wilson positioned herself as guardian of the sick room and would allow no one but herself and Dr. Cary Grayson in the room. Dr. Francis Dercum and Dr. Hugh Young were called as consultants. Even Robert Lansing, secretary of state, and Thomas Marshall, vice president, were not informed of the true nature of Wilson's illness. Mrs. Wilson kept presidential aides out of the sick room for several months, and at times gave her own answers to policy questions in the margin of documents, as if they came from Wilson himself.[19]

James Polk had in Sarah a close associate who shared his beliefs and, in many cases, may have felt more strongly about his policies than he did. There has been no first lady who lent the advice and support to the presidency as Sarah did. Eleanor Roosevelt was very influential during FDR's administration, but she had her own agenda. Eleanor was involved more in social concerns than in national governmental policy. She was away from the White House quite often and for long periods of time and so was FDR, but they did not often travel together. Since Eleanor and Franklin occupied separate sleeping quarters, it does not seem possible that there was substantial dialogue between them. Between Sarah and James Polk there was undoubtedly a lot of pillow talk about the matters of state.[20]

Sarah was the most outspoken and the most active of first ladies in politics since Abigail Adams. However, Abigail interested herself in matters for which Sarah showed no particular concern: women's rights. On March 31, 1776, she wrote to her husband as follows:

> *I have sometimes been to think that the passion for liberty cannot be equally strong in the breasts of those who are accustomed to deprive their fellow creatures of theirs. I am certain that it is not founded upon that generous and Christian practice of doing to others as we would that others do to us. ...*
>
> *I long to hear that you have declared an independence, and by the way, in the new code of laws which I suppose will be necessary for you to make, I desire that you remember the ladies, and be more generous and favorable to these than your ancestors. Do not put such unlimited power in the hands of the husbands. Remember all men would be tyrants if they could. If particular care is not paid to the ladies, we are determined to forment a rebellion [sic] and will not hold ourselves bound to any laws in which we have no voice or representation. That your sex is naturally tyrannical is a truth so thoroughly established as to admit of no dispute.[21]*

This was strong language for a woman in Adams's time. She seemed to have very strong opinions about many things, including the tea boycott. She apparently was concerned at times with policies on her husband's agenda.

Sarah, with few exceptions, lent herself to giving her full support to her husband's bold and visionary program of national expansion. Polk's letters to Sarah were strong proof that he withheld nothing from her and that he was eager to have her opinion in all matters. Sarah's opinions were sought, not imposed. A New York newspaper called the first lady "a most auspicious domestic influence and the President's guardian angel." Polk himself said, "None but Sarah knew so intimately my private affairs."

Polk very often paid tribute publicly to Sarah's wisdom. He is felt to have depended upon her advice as he did no other. He never consulted, as did General Jackson, a kitchen cabinet of trusted personal advisers. Polk often could not, and did not, rely on his cabinet for advice. However, it was important that husband and wife maintain secrecy about the strong influence that Sarah exerted through her husband on the governmental process.[22]

On one occasion guests in the White House found the first lady reading a current novel. The guests were surprised that she, with all of her other activities, could find time to read fiction. Sarah informed them that she had many books presented to her and that she tried to read them all, but she admitted that it was impossible to read everything. However, on that evening the author of the book she was reading was dining with the president, and she could not be so unkind as to appear wholly ignorant and uninformed of his gift.[23]

In July 1846 Andrew Johnson's relations with Polk were strained. Johnson was a hungry congressman from Tennessee who felt that he was not getting his fair share of appointments for his supporters in that state. On July 23, 1846, he wrote to Blackston McDannel: "Take Polk's appointments all in all and they are the most damnable set that was ever made by any president since the government was organized out of Tennessee as well as in it."

However, Johnson's assessment of Polk was not a fair one. Polk was aloof and rigid in his policies and did not seem to wish to curry favor with party members. Johnson lamented, "The democracy in my district ... seems to have fallen under the political displeasure of the administration." However, Martha Johnson, the congressman's wife, was a frequent White House guest of Mrs. Polk. Sarah, having no children of her own, took a great interest in the children of Tennesseans who were in the government.

Sarah was described as being a formidable lady in her own right. "Endowed with regal stateliness and conscious of possessing the most high-toned manners, she personified what one admirer called 'the aristocracy of virtue'; an idea that, whatever the mass of society might consider themselves at liberty to do, it was indispensable, due to her station, to preserve inviolate the strict laws of decorum and of the purest principles." Someone said in praise of Sarah that she had never been known to "discuss a subject in relation to which her sex was expected to be ignorant."[24]

One topic on which Sarah and Martha Johnson agreed was housekeeping. The White House during the previous occupancy had deteriorated to a sad state. The White House was described as having become slatternly: "Cheese was smeared on the upholstery in the East Room, and tobacco spital bespeckled the Turkish carpets."[25]

Perhaps some small part of the Southerner's idea of the role of women in society resided in Sarah and kept her from being openly assertive about politics. Women along with children and slaves were expected to recognize their proper and subordinate place and to be obedient to the head of the family. Any tendency on the part of the members of the system to assert themselves against the master threatened the whole, and therefore the system of slavery itself. It is no accident that the most articulate spokesmen for slavery were also eloquent espousers of the subordinate role of women.[26]

Many politicians and officials were aware of Sarah's great influence over her husband. James Buchanan, while touring with the president, wrote to Sarah, "We have gotten along as could be expected in your absence." Henry Clay, a political opponent, told Sarah that everyone agreed in commending her excellent administration, and Sarah responded that she was glad to hear that her administration was popular.[27]

The geniality of the first lady obscured her remarkable political acumen. She had, without it being apparent, broken the mold of convention that had cast the female in the role of being decorative and domestic. A few admirers described her as being beautiful, while others used the term "elegant" and "queenly." A good friend of Martin Van Buren, Henry Gilpin, said that he was much impressed with "the good lady who is presiding at the White House." He described her as "really a very superior person," that time had "dealt generously with her personal charms and if she is not handsome, she is at least prepossessing and graceful, dresses with taste and is extremely affable as well as perfectly self-possessed." He further stated that if he was not mistaken she "has both sagacity and decision that would make her a good counselor in some emergencies."[28]

Gilpin was a strong supporter of both Jackson and Van Buren. He was greatly admired by Jackson after he gave a strong antibank speech Polk had published in the Columbia papers and later republished in the Nashville papers.[29]

The tendency of men to confide their affairs, even their love affairs, to Sarah was most unusual. A letter from Congressman Samuel Mardis of Alabama, dated October 4, 1834, and addressed to J. K. Polk, refers to a new daughter recently born to his wife.

... and if you will shut your eyes and stop your ears; I will tell Mrs. Polk privately what has happened since our arrival. Of that she could see the beautiful plump little creature, my feelings overcome me; I cannot prosecute the matter farther. Its name is Samuel Yates Mardis. ... This leaves my constituents in good humor as it does Mary Eliza, children, and myself in good health. What about [sic] will you go and when will you start? Mary Eliza sends her love to all and talks of meeting her in Washington at times; not positive. Let me hear from you soon.

Sam. W. Mardis[30]

Mardis, who was elected to Congress twice, was, like Polk, strongly pro–Jackson.

James Polk received a letter from a long-time confidante, Arkansas's Congressman Archibald Yell, on June 24, 1842, but most of the letter was directed to Sarah, whom he supposed had an attentive ear. The wording suggests that Sarah was again in the role of matchmaker:

If I should be pleased with Mrs. Polk's widdow [sic] and she with me, she may talk me back to old Tennessee. Would not that present a strange history in my life, and who knows but it may happen [sic] I am now quite in love with the widdow [sic], and if I am not mistaken in her appearance, for I knew her in 1827, she is large fine looking and she must be available. Her father was one of the best men who ever lived. Tell Mrs. Polk she has set me half crazy, and now I cannot abandon the claim until the matter is further investigated. But my dear sis, I am up to near forty, and she cannot be older than 33 or 35 at fartherest. She will be detered [sic] too, from this land of the Bowie knives, I fear, and aga[in] how presumptious [sic] of me to make a tour to Tennessee to see a lady with some hope or expectation of success.

Say to Mrs. Polk — or you must give me a minute detail of her appearance, intelligence, age, and no. of children, and such other particulars as may interest me. Old widdowers [sic] are the greatest fools on earth; I shall therefore close this subject. Let me hear from you and how things progress.[31]

Somewhat later Yell, in a letter to Polk, advised Sarah about the progress of his courtship of the said widow. The letter was dated October 31, 1843. Congressman Yell wrote that he was still single: "That I am not disposed to quarrel with old friends but that I consider that she has fed me on hope and expectations so long that I am not sure that I can now marry at all. A widdow [*sic*] is my choice and rather to be thought very fastidious, I will take that one which is left, but I ought to have had first choice. Still situated as I am in the matter I believe I prefer the one that is unmarried. She is a good democrat and a fine splendid looking woman and about the proper age. I am as ever, Yell."[32]

Buchanan, the bachelor president, and his bachelor associate, William King of Alabama, shared quarters with each other for over 30 years in Washington. Buchanan's associates were largely Southerners who usually left their wives at home and lived in hotels or boarding houses where the occupants were largely male. Their wives, as wives do everywhere, were bound to speculate on the life and activities of the lonely bachelor. Over many years Buchanan's roommate and close friend was a senator and later vice president. Such an association was certain to spawn gossip. Once in a letter to Sarah, Aaron Brown of Tennessee referred to Buchanan and King as "man and wife." All evidence indicates, however, that Buchanan remained celibate as well as unmarried. He was not recorded as having expressed any great loss due to his bachelor state.[33]

Sarah's character and temperament were multifaceted. Evidence is found in a letter from Judge Lewis of Lancaster, Pennsylvania:

> *On the fourth of July, 1846, the President's mansion was thrown open for the reception of visitors and the rooms gradually filled with guests of high and low degree. Amid the motley group present, the first lady was receiving with becoming courtesy the guests who advanced to pay their respects, when she perceived an old man supported by a lone cane, and dressed in humble garb tottering into the room and in a diffident manner take a station at a distance and gazed with unmingled wonder upon the scene before him. Mrs. Polk dispatched a gentleman with whom she was then conversing to bring the old man to her, and talked with him for some time with a kindly sympathy for old age which is a beautiful feature of a woman's character. He said he was 108 years old, had dined with Washington, and his memory reached thirty years beyond the stirring events of the American Revolution. His reminiscences of bygone times were received with attention by his auditors and when other guests claimed her ear she followed the old man with her eye and directed that the venerable visitor should be treated with special respect.*[34]

At one time a party of young ladies pleaded with Sarah to let them dance in the White House. But Sarah was adamant, and asked the young ladies if they would think of dancing in such a public place as the White House. Sarah went on to say that she would not have dancing in these rooms because it would be undignified, and it would be respectful neither to the house nor to the office. "How indecorous it would seem for dancing to be going on in one apartment," she said, "while in another we were conversing with dignitaries of the republics or ministers of the gospel."[35]

Sarah's Sabbatarianism and her attitude toward certain activities grew out of her environment. When Mrs. Felix Grundy, a social arbiter and wife of James Polk's one-time law partner, had tried to start a Sunday School in Nashville, the idea was denounced as a desecration of the Sabbath. The social acceptance of dancing in Nashville was delayed for many years. When the Reverend C. A. Elliott, the principal of the Female Academy, introduced instruction in dancing into the curriculum, the press strongly denounced his action. The Nashville *Christian Advocate*, a publication of the Methodist church, denounced the action as "vain, foolish, and profitless," and it was at this time that Sarah put an end to dancing in the White House.[36]

Sarah was known for her disdain of hard liquor. It has been written that there was no drinking of alcoholic beverages in the White House during the Polk administration. Such was not the case. All that the first lady prohibited was hard liquor. However, Washington was a hard-drinking town, and Sarah's ban made many people in the district unhappy. Sarah probably objected to the use of hard drink because she did not think that such practice was proper in the White House. It is significant that the temperance movement was afloat in the 1840s, which may have influenced Sarah's actions. She set an example by not serving strong drink.

The Polks did serve wine. Sarah had to stock her wine cellar with table wines, champagne for desserts, and after-dinner brandy. Table wine was purchased by the barrel and was a significant part of the White House expenses.[37]

Sarah, as well as many friends of the Polks, was concerned about the president's health. His frail and sickly appearance and his long working hours were partially a consequence of his failure to delegate or assign work to anyone except Sarah. The president had little trust in those who surrounded him in his administration and the sole person to whom he confided and called on for help and advice was his wife. In June 1845 Sarah received a letter from an old friend, Judge John Catron, who cautioned her about James's working habits:

We had the pleasure to hear by Mrs. Marshall's letter that you were very well and the president not overworked, of course. On this lead I am uneasy and advise lectures on your part on all inordinate and especially irregular labors. The machinery of government looks well at a distance, smooth, still, and statesman-like. I think the president was deeply impressed on his early copy set him in the old field schoolhouse, "less said is sooner mended." It is worth more in practice than all ever written in Italy and France on slippery policy. All sides seem to vie in vaunting you and if this keeps up through the four years will stilt you up to so giddy a height that you may incur more danger in getting down than climbing up.[38]

On Saturday, September 20, 1845, Polk noted in his diary as follows:

The Cabinet met today and it being the regular day of the meeting all the members were present. Nothing of importance occurred. The President announced his intention to appoint the Honorable Levi Woodberry to be judge of the Superior Court of the US in place of Judge Story, deceased. All the members of the Cabinet cordially approved the appointment. Andrew J. Donelson [Rachel Jackson's nephew and Jackson's ward], Esquire, late chargé d'affaires, visited the President today and spent some time in conversation with the President and Cabinet on Texas and Mexican affairs. Mr. Donelson was in feeble health and on the President's invitation he was put up in a room in the president's mansion.[39]

On Sunday, September 21, 1845, Polk noted: "The President and Mrs. Polk attended the First Presbyterian Church today. Mr. Donelson was quite ill today and was confined to his chamber all day. I sent for Dr. Miller in the afternoon who prescribed for him. At about 1:20 o'clock P.M. and shortly after the President and his family returned from church a servant brought the President the card of the Honorable Daniel Jennitras, late minister of the US to Austria; and Mr. [Edward A.] Hannegan, US Senator from Indiana."[40]

The Polks, this time as always, took care of their own. Andrew Jackson Donelson, ward of the old general, was to Sarah and James one of their many surrogate children whom Polk sheltered throughout his administration.

Just before Christmas 1845, the Polks invited all the judges of the Supreme Court to a dinner. The invitation read: "The President and

Mrs. Polk request the pleasure of your company to dinner on Friday inst. at 5 P.M."

Sarah's attire on this occasion was as usual very impressive. Her dress was a dark blue velvet dress with Brussels lace trimming at the neck and under the sleeves to match a long Brussels lace scarf worn around her neck and reaching nearly to the floor. The sleeves were confined at the wrists by scarlet bracelets which matched the scarlet cashmere turban embroidered in gold and trimmed with gold fringe which covered her jet black curls.[41]

The guests were received in the circular Blue Room, where the decor blended well with her attire. The 40 guests were seated in her dining room: the West Room of the right wing. The furnishings were new and the decorations had been recently installed. This was one of the rooms that Sarah had refurbished soon after becoming first lady. The three long windows were decorated with purple- and gold-figured curtains, and the dining table was circled with purple velvet chairs with carved rosewood frames.

The servants were dressed in dark blue coats, white vests, cravats, and gloves. All blended well with the furnishings. The table itself had a center ornament of gilt-burnished vases of flowers that made a brilliant splash of color, and around this were 200 chandeliers, candelabra, and figures. The china was marine gold with marine blue and gold and an eagle crest, and the dessert plates were marine blue and gold with fruits and flowers painted in the center. The meal was served in courses: soup, fish, canvas-back duck, turkey, green peas, spinach, garnished ham, côtelettes de mouton, potatoes shaped in a ball, croquettes poulet, paté de foie, jellies, orange and lemon charlotte russe, ices, pink mud oranges, prunes, and sweet meats.[42]

At one of Sarah's parties, a congressman remarked, "This is a very genteel affair," and Sarah, not smiling, said, "I have never seen it otherwise."[43]

Chapter 6

From the start of their sojourn in the White House the Polks discussed matters of great national import when all of their company had gone. There were many problems to deal with and both aired their opinions freely. In one of their face-to-face talks, James told Sarah that there were four major objectives that he wished to pursue: (1) the reduction in the tariff; (2) the independent treasury; (3) the settlement of the Oregon question; and (4) the acquisition of California.[1]

Sarah, showing the depth of her knowledge concerning the affairs of state, asked, "What about the question of Texas?" James answered, "I regard that as already settled." Later events were to show that this was far from true.

"I want to give all my attention to the Oregon question," James said. "It is ours by right of settlement. It has been ten years since the Methodist missionaries established the first permanent settlement in the Willamette Valley, and hundreds of American settlers have gone to Oregon each year, but two years ago about a thousand people traveled the Oregon Trail to settle in the valley also. We have more people there than the British do." And then James stated with some heat, "I partially based my campaign for the presidency on the idea that the region belonged to the United States. Now war threatens us over the territory. I will accept no terms other than the 49th parallel as the dividing line between us."[2]

Polk's Indian policy was essentially a continuation of that initiated and carried out by Andrew Jackson. In September 1845 Polk held three conferences with delegates from six nations of Indians. Polk heard their grievances and their wish to mediate. There were the usual ceremonial gifts from the Indians. Mrs. Polk was presented with a beaded bag, and a beaded pocketbook was presented to the president, both from a Tuscarora chief. The gifts had been made by the chief's wife. On the next day, after Sarah chided Polk, he presented the chief with a shawl for his wife and a gold pin for himself. In addition, Polk promised $100 for the Indians to pay their expenses for the trip to Washington. Polk reported that the Indians had addressed him as their great father and Sarah as their great mother.[3]

Jackson's policy toward the Indians in America was a continuation of an Old World precedent by which the weaker was pushed out of territory desired by the stronger. Actually, the same type of excuses for misplacing the less strong dates back to biblical times: "The country is a land for cattle," said the children of Reuben to Moses when they saw the land of Gilead, and thy servants have cattle; wherefore, said they, if we have found grace in thy sight, let this land be given unto thy servants for a possession."[4]

Historian Samuel Eliot Morrison writes: "In the United States, as elsewhere in the nineteenth century, this process of conquest and expansion took the form of a relatively highly developed civilization pushing out a backward people who could not or would not be absorbed, and who were too few in number and weak in technique long to resist."[5]

It was after Andrew Jackson became president that Georgia, Alabama, and Mississippi, all showing disregard for federal treaties, assumed control of Indian reservations. They even went so far as to form county governments that were to be enforced as soon as the natives were expelled.

Jackson, in his farewell address of 1837, provided a justification for his treatment of the Indians: "The states which had so long been retarded in their improvement by the Indian tribes residing in the midst of them are at length relieved from the evil, and this unhappy race — the original dwellers in our land, are now placed in a situation where we may well hope that they will share in the blessings of civilization."[6]

The Jackson policy toward the Indians did not end with the old general. Polk, late in his administration in an annual message to Congress, boasted of eight Indian treaties that resulted in the U.S. government acquiring more than 18.5 million acres of land. This acquisition, vast in scope, served to permit whites to move into large new areas. Polk also continued Jackson's policy of Indian removal. The Polk administration disrupted the native tribal jurisdiction over their affairs by declaring that the Commission of Indian Affairs could supervise the expenditure of Indian funds.[7]

Jackson stated his true belief with regard to the Indian question when he wrote, "I thought with the ancient Romans that it was never right to cede any land or boundary of the republic, but always to add to it by honorable treaty, thus extending the area of freedom. ... The annexation of Texas to the United States promises to enlarge the circle of free institutions."[8] Thus, "extending the area of freedom" became, along with manifest destiny, the battle cry for the Jackson and later the Polk administration. It is felt that Jackson meant to equate freedom with the Republic, that is the United States. Texas was a Republican state and was recognized by the Jackson administration.[9]

Polk betrayed his ideas of what place the Indians should aspire to in society. It had been earlier the practice to fund schooling for the natives in various states, but Polk, through William Medill, began a new policy that prescribed opportunity for education only in Indian lands and decreed that, in general, the only training should be in manual labor.[10]

The American people of Sarah's time and later have employed peculiar rationalization for the manner in which they achieved their good fortunes and extended their boundaries. Readers during the Polk era found these words in John Higginson's *An Early New England Preacher:*

> Thou God hath blessed lo his poor people and they have increased here from low beginnings to great estates that the Lord may call his whole generation to witness. Oh! Generation see! Look upon your towns and fields, look upon your habitations, crops and ships, and behold your numerous posterity and in great increase in blessings of land and sea. Have I been a wilderness to you? We must need answer, no, Lord thou has been a gracious God and exceeding good to thy servants even in these earthly blessings. We live in a more comfortable and plentiful manner than we ever did expect.

From that day to this it remains difficult to recognize the fortuitous and the providential element in our good fortune. If either moral pride or the spirit of nationalism tries to draw every element in an historic situation into rational coherence — and persuades us to establish a direct congruity between our good fortune or our virtue or skill — we will inevitably claim more for our contribution to our prosperity than the facts will warrant. This has remained a source of confusion in American life.[11]

Sarah Polk held very similar views to that of her husband on the matters of slavery and the treatment of Indians. She felt that both were predestined to their roles in life. There was a popular expression current during Polk's years as president: "Extension of the area of freedom." This saying was a partial definition of manifest destiny and was to become the key phrase for expansionism.[12]

In the 1840s the term "manifest destiny" suited the mood and spirit of the American nation. Assumed to be preordained and blessed from heaven, the extent of expansion meant different things to different persons. To some it meant expansion to the Pacific; to others it meant the whole North American continent. It had become such a popular concept by the mid–1840s that it became a movement to offer, in a spirit of idealism, the opportunity for self-realization.[13] The doors to the temple of freedom must be made open to people who were panting for freedom. Any shrinking from admitting them, out of selfish disinclination to share with others the blessings of freedom, would be disgraceful. If it grew out of the fear of consequences, we should meekly take the badge of dishonor and pin it to our front.[14]

The Polk administration embraced and nourished the idea of manifest destiny and extending the area of freedom. James Polk, by belief and by training, was admirably suited to fulfill the mission of extending this area. Polk's ideas of American virtue and superiority had been formed in college during that early heyday of nationalism and expansionism following the War of 1812.[15]

Movements need slogans and Polk may have been inspired by an article in the *Democratic Review* written by John Sullivan in July 1845 in which he brought forward his belief concerning westward expansion of the nation: "It is our manifest destiny to overspread the continent and possess the whole continent which Providence has given us for the development of the great experiment of liberty and federated self government entrusted to us."[16]

The annexation of Texas, admitted as the twenty-eighth state on December 29, 1845, increased Polk's popularity. Indeed, expansion was the main accomplishment of the Polk administration.[17] Then on May 13, 1846, the United States formally declared war against Mexico.

To those who opposed the war, it was aggression on the part of the United States. Abraham Lincoln, a congressman from Illinois, brought into question the moral justification of the war. He wanted Polk to outline precisely the spot upon which U.S. soil had been invaded by the Mexicans. Lincoln was implying that it was the Americans who had unjustly provoked the Mexicans into entering the war.[18]

Lincoln felt that the United States was wrong on moral grounds in waging war with Mexico. He argued that Polk's claim that the Rio Grande was the true border between the two countries was based on pure speculation. In an address before Congress he stated, "Whenever the House is desirous to obtain a full knowledge of all the facts which go to establish whether the particular spot of soil on which the blood of our citizens was so shed, was or was it not at that time our own soil?"[19] Lincoln was declaring that the United States had provoked a war with Mexico without first establishing a claim about the true line of demarcation.

Once started, the conflict was presumed by the majority of U.S. citizens to be a just war, and the attitude of Sarah seems to have been that since the United States was engaged in a war, Americans must not have scruples about how it was started or by whom.

Sarah was most likely influential in her husband's determination to expand to the southwest and westward to the Pacific. The doctrine of manifest destiny, supported by the president and the first lady, was part of their Calvinist belief that it was foreordained by God that the United States was chosen to occupy those lands.[20]

Sarah became a good friend of General Gideon Pillow, a fellow townsman of Polk, whose command had been engaged with distinction at Vera Cruz. As a delegate at the Baltimore convention, he had played a significant role in Polk's nomination for president. General Pillow gave Sarah an expensive pearl pin. She was also given by General Worth a portrait of Hernando Cortés, first conqueror of Mexico. There is some policy inconsistency here since James and Sarah had been rather adamant in general in their refusal of expensive gifts.[21]

At the onset of the Mexican War, the cabinet and the president were photographed by an unknown daguerreotypist, when the technique was less than ten years old. The picture is the first one known to be taken inside the White House. This picture, very much faded, has survived in Sarah Polk's keepsakes. Mrs. Polk had summoned a daguerreotypist to be present after a cabinet breakfast. She did this as a means of tricking Attorney General John Mason into being included in the picture. She had privately tried to get Mason to sit for a picture but he had refused. Sarah, however, was not one to give up. Mason, teasing the first lady, behaved like a little boy; he slouched in his chair and leaned to one side with a cocky expression on his face. He would not concede to have his head put in a clamp as was almost required in long-term exposure to prevent blurring. The other cabinet members were cooperative and are shown as models of order. James Polk was seated in front and on either side of him were "moon-faced" William Marcy, the secretary of war, and the frail little Robert Walker, secretary of the treasury. In the rear, standing, were two younger men, Postmaster General Cave Johnson, and George Bancroft. James Buchanan was not present.[22]

Sarah regarded the results of the Mexican War — that is, the addition of California and New Mexico to U.S. territory — as among the most important events in the history of the country. She recognized that there were some who were opposed to this acquisition and she brushed them off saying that there was always someone opposed to everything.[23]

For the duration of the Mexican War, dinners in the White House were not given for festivity. The parties after the onset of the war were devoted to politics, war news, and personal ambition.[24]

One of the topics of discussion was that of retaliation at the Rio Grande. A dinner party guest recalled how Sarah expressed her sentiments:

> At no period in our history have we seen the hospitality more handsomely dispensed or displayed with more Republican simplicity. There is no extra formality when a secretary or some other officer of government presents himself. The quiet unheralded citizen receives a polite and cordial salutation as well as the rich man or the ministers of state. I was struck with Mrs. Polk's patriotic sentiments. A gallant lieutenant just back from the bloody but glorious conflict at Monterey was there also; and as she carried back his thoughts to the distant field of his fame he caught the inspirations, and dealt briefly upon some of the thrilling incidents of those scenes. In the course of this animated conversation, the young officer remarked that something — I do not now recollect what — was rather too democratic; to which Mrs. Polk replied that whatever sustained the honor and advanced the interests of the country, whether regarded as democratic or not, she admired and applauded.[25]

The waging of the Mexican War imposed a terrible strain on Polk's constitution. He was in poor health to begin with, and his long, arduous working hours caused a further decline of his physical powers. During the four years the Polks spent in the White House, they took only a few days of vacation.[26]

James's health was one of Sarah's chief concerns, and she tried to urge him to get more rest. Through the era of expansion and the Mexican War, Polk had labored night and day and, as was his habit, had delegated no important duties except to Sarah. The first lady had seen her husband fight many tough political battles before and survive the strain. She was aware that he would persist even if it meant losing his life in the attempt. Sarah tried to hide her anxiety and strove even harder to lighten his load. But throughout his presidency he would trust no one but her to share his burdens.[27]

Polk continued to work without respite, in spite of the toll it was taking on his infirm body. Sarah chided him. She told him that he could not bear this heavy load indefinitely, and that he could not go on working day and night, month after month. But James insisted that the work had to be done. On one occasion Sarah reminded him that it was 2 A.M. before he had gone to bed the night before and 3 A.M. the night before that. Polk reminded her that there was no remedy for it unless she could persuade people to take a long nap every day and then go to bed at sundown. He then added that it appeared he was not expected to do any work until everyone else was asleep.

The president was rapidly depleting whatever physical reserves he may have had. He was trying with his waning strength to achieve all of the goals he had set for himself in his campaign. He had, in his distrust of others, failed to delegate even the most minor details of his work. He told Sarah that he could not rest until he had made good all of his election promises. But Sarah kept after him, telling him that he could not go on in the present manner, that he was as thin as a string and so tired that he could not eat, and so nervous that he could not sleep. She begged him to take a holiday, for her sake. James responded by promising Sarah that just as soon as Congress adjourned they would take a little trip.[28]

Polk had a long and difficult struggle with Congress over a bill that he had introduced in an attempt to shorten the Mexican War. He had made a request for an appropriation of $2 million dollars to be used in negotiating a treaty with Mexico. According to Polk, the chief difficulty would be, in establishing a boundary, and in adjusting the boundary the United States should pay a fair equivalent for every concession that must be made by Mexico.[29]

During a recess of the Congress, a number of unhappy northerners discussed the question of slavery and its possible expansion if more territory were to be acquired. In what followed was a prolonged filibuster: the first significant one. Polk's $2 million bill was defeated and he was very disappointed.[30]

This long battle in Congress took its toll and the president took the promised vacation.

James wrote in his diary as follows:

> On Wednesday, August 18, 1846, this morning at 9:00 I went aboard the steamer Osceola with Mrs. Polk, her niece, Mrs. Rucker [Johanna] and two servants to take an excursion to Fortress Monroe. We took with us two servants, Major E. P. McNeal, his wife, daughter, and Mrs. Williams, the sister of Mrs. McNeal, all of Tennessee, who had been a day or two at the presidential mansion. My intention is to take an excursion of only two to three days. It is my first absence from Washington since I have been President, except for a single day in the spring of 1845 when I visited Mount Vernon, going and returning the same day. My long confinement to my office had considerably enfeebled me and rendered some recreation necessary. After having looked into the laws passed by the last session of Congress and given the necessary directions for carrying them into effect, no public interest I think will suffer from my absence for a few [days]. All the members of the Cabinet agree to remain at their posts except Judge Mason, the Attorney General, who at my request accompanied me. At 9:00 I went aboard the Osceola and I found the Secretaries of Treasury, War and Navy at the steamboat. They accompanied me as far as Alexandria and returned to Washington. The passage down the Potomac was a pleasant one. Before dark the wind rose and after passing the mouth of the Potomac we found the bay very rough and almost everyone on board was affected by seasickness. Mrs. Polk, Mrs. Rucker, Mrs. McNeal were very sick too. I was not myself sick.[31]

There are a number of things found in this letter that are characteristic of the man Sarah married. Why does a loving husband refer to his wife as Mrs. Polk instead of Sarah? This labels him as a stiff, formal person. Here is a man who has labored 18 months for incredibly long hours, who seems in one voice to be both apologetic and boastful that he had taken only a part of a day's vacation in that time.

Also, oddly, this man who was taking only a few days of vacation took time to write several long, tedious, boring letters that must have consumed hours of his time.

At Fortress Monroe he was beset by hordes of well-wishers. He did, between greeting long lines of visitors, have a chance to walk around

on the beach and view the fortification, but one day he was carried off
to Norfolk on what he described as one of the hottest days. In Norfolk
he had to survive long hours of handshaking, dining, and parading in
the hot sun. Following that exhausting day, he spent a restless, sleep-
less night. The next morning he was quite ill, but he compelled himself to entertain a guest.

In Polk's diary notation for Friday, August 21, 1846, he described
something of his ordeal during his visit to Norfolk on the third day of
his visit:

> On reaching the navy yard a salute was fired from the ship Pennsyl-
> vania and a cutter, which were laying at anchor near the yard. Our
> party was conducted on board the Pennsylvania where I was received by
> Commodore Wilkinson and the naval officers attached to this station.
> After examining the fine ship, we were conducted on shore, examined
> the dry dock, and were conducted from there on foot through a boiling
> sun (being one of the hottest days of the season). The hotel was situated
> more than a fourth of a mile from the wharf where we landed. On
> reaching it, I found a large crowd assembled. I was conducted into a
> parlor where I was introduced to several hundred people. I was almost
> overcome from excessive heat, for it was one of hottest days I ever felt,
> but still I made an effort and endured the fatigue though it was any-
> thing but pleasant to me. The ladies had been conducted to a different
> apartment in the hotel. After remaining in the hotel one hour or more,
> constantly on my feet, receiving and shaking hands with persons who
> were introduced to me, I spoke of returning to the steamer, when to my
> surprise that I learned that a dinner was being prepared. This I regret-
> ted as my fatigue and suffering from heat were very great. However,
> there was no alternative but to remain or to act with seeming rude-
> ness — I found myself on return to Fortress Monroe in the evening
> greatly fatigued and perfectly wet with perspiration.[32]

Polk's so-called vacation at Fortress Monroe had done nothing to
improve the president's physical state. Fortress Monroe had not proved
to be a haven. It was a place teeming with visitors. He had left one set
of visitors behind in the capital only to encounter a new hoard of callers.
On the day of departure for Washington, the president was suffering
from abdominal discomfort, fever, and an aching body. Polk was very
ill but he got out of bed in order to keep Sarah from worrying. She was
not fooled, and urged him to go back to bed. James protested that his
problem was no more than a cold and too much sun. The president
rested on a sofa all day, too weak and ill to rise and greet visitors.

In a day or two the fever abated, but Sarah was still very concerned about his condition and she urged him to remain for another week to recover. But James protested, as he felt compelled to return to the capital for an important meeting, and he pointed out that Washington was perhaps more restful than Fortress Monroe.[33]

Sarah's friendliness and social graces made up to some degree for James's austerity. He seemed to be without humor and was very cold and formal in dealing with the public. He had a difficult relationship with his top generals, Winfield Scott and Zachary Taylor. While Lincoln did not seem to care at all about his generals' habits and politics as long as they won battles, Polk quarreled with Scott and Taylor, even though they won battles with regularity. Polk felt their successes on the battlefield were causing them to aspire to the presidency.[34]

During the war, Polk was unpopular with many in New England who viewed the conflict as a means of expanding slavery. Sarah, however, remained popular with the majority. At a White House reception a Southern visitor was heard to say, "Madam, I have long wished to look upon a lady upon whom the Bible pronounces a woe." Those gathered became exceedingly quiet, not knowing what to expect next. The answer soon followed.

"Does not the Bible say, 'Woe unto you when all men speak well of you'?"[35]

Fortunately for Polk, Sarah was there to soften his stiff, cold manner. Despite her rigorous attitude toward dancing, cards, and hard drink, she remained popular. She read a great deal and was able to make suitable comments on what she read. In spite of her insistence that they must keep their expenses within Polk's salary of $35,000, she was able to dress elegantly.[36]

There are those who feel that Polk was very dull, and that the only thing he knew was work and more work. We have only rare evidence that he possessed any humor. Indeed, Sarah must have been very fond of him or she would not have tolerated a man who was so obsessed with ambition. His diaries are dull, tedious, and wordy. The most astounding thing about his diaries is his ceaseless repetition of "I" and the fact that the person who was his mainstay and only confidante is mentioned only in connection with a severe illness that she suffered while in the White House. He was such a workaholic that he seemed apologetic when recording his August 1846 excursion outside of Washington to Fortress Monroe. An equally pathetic revelation is that he spent Christmas Day of that same year working in his office while Sarah attended church.[39]

It is amazing, indeed, that some biographer has not feasted on the James Polk story and written a psychobiography, such as Pierce Clark's study of Lincoln or Edwin Winstein's profile of Wilson's neurological illness. What sort of profile would have been written about a man who worked all day, even on Christmas Eve, who almost never took a vacation, who trusted almost no one, and who confided in almost no one? This humorless man of overweening ambition, who delegated almost no authority, was reluctant to note that anyone other than himself had in any way contributed to his success.

A psychiatrist would probably say that Polk possessed a paranoid and compulsive personality, but was not an outright psychopath. It was indeed a testimony to Sarah's devotion and emotional stability that she remained with James and loved him for 25 years.

Many clinical features of paranoid personality were noted in Polk's behavior. Individuals with this disorder have a pervasive and inappropriate mistrust of others. They assume that others intend to harm, exploit, or trick them. Thus they may question, without justification, the loyalty or trustworthiness of friends or sexual partners. They are reluctant to confide in others for fear the information will be used against them, they appear guarded and tense, and they constantly scan their environment for clues of possible attack, deception, or betrayal. They often find evidence of such malevolence by misinterpreting non-events (such as a glance in their direction) as demeaning and threatening. In response to perceived or actual insults or betrayals, these individuals overreact, quickly becoming excessively angry and responding with counterattacking behavior. They are unable to forgive or forget and bear longtime grudges against their supposed betrayers. Some are litigious. Whereas some individuals would appear intensely aloof and hostile, others are overly angry and combative. A person with this disorder is usually socially isolated, and because of their paranoia often have difficulties with coworkers.[38]

While James Polk did at times project as cold and austere, there was one person who could distract him from his almost ceaseless labors. Some extracts from his diary are revealing:

> *Sunday, May 2, 1847*
> *I was indisposed this morning from the effects of cold, and much*

fatigued from the labor of the past week and remained quietly at home. It was, moreover, a damp uncomfortable day and unusually chilly for the season. Mrs. Polk and Mrs. Rucker, her niece, attended church. The quiet rest of the Sabbath Day is always desirable to me, but has seldom been more acceptable than on this day. When Mrs. Polk returned from church she complained of being very cold, and it was manifest she had a chill, and a short time later a reaction took place and she had a fever. She had slight symptoms of a chill Friday last, which had not attracted much attention as she had casually mentioned it, but had not complained of much indisposition and consequence of it.[39]

On Tuesday, May 4, 1847, there is another entry in Polk's diary:

I rose this morning as usual about 6 o'clock and while I was shaving in my chambers (for I am my own barber) Mrs. Polk, who had not arisen, asked me if it was a cool morning and complained of being very cold. I answered her that I thought it was more chilly than usual. I soon discovered that she had a chill, and threw more covering on the bed. Her chill continued for more than three hours. I have never seen her suffer or complain more than she did for several hours. After the chill subsided the fever rose. My family physician [Dr. Miller] I learned was absent from the city. I sent for Dr. Hall, who is one of the most eminent physicians in the city, and he prescribed for her. She spent a restless and uncomfortable afternoon and night. Though her medicine had its desired effect.[40]

From Polk's description of Sarah's illness, it is almost certain that she had malaria. The timing and sequence of the chills and fever occurring at 48-eight hour intervals would label the type of malaria as tertiary, caused by plasmodium vivax. Though the type of treatment was not mentioned, there was effective treatment for malaria in Polk's time. As early as 1786, George Washington's private physician, Dr. James Craik, treated him for the first time with Peruvian or Jesuits bark, a substance that contained quinine and achieved excellent results. Quinine, the active agent of Peruvian bark, was not isolated until 1820. As early as 1776 the extract of Peruvian bark had been used on the colonial troops and it is quite odd that Craik did not use the bark earlier.[41] It seems, however, that Sarah's treatment had not been adequate or prolonged enough because on Sunday, May 9, 1847, the president noted in his diary: "Mrs. Polk has been closely confined to her chamber for several days past by a violent attack of intermittent fever but she is much better today."[42]

In May 1847 Polk refused to allow gas illumination of the federal buildings in Washington to commemorate military victories in Mexico. His reasoning was that such illumination might present a fire hazard to the buildings and their stores of public records. He did, however, permit the White House and the homes of the heads of executive departments to be lit. It was Sarah who reminded the president that the public records might be damaged by fire. But she added, "I was glad that you allowed our house to be illuminated. All of the heads of departments are lighting their respective residences and many of the houses in the city are illuminated."[43]

At Sarah's urging Polk had another portrait done. The Dialectic Society of the University of North Carolina had requested the portrait to be done for the debating hall. The university had hired Mr. Sully, a famous American artist to come from Philadelphia to do the portrait.[44]

In the spring of 1847 Polk received an invitation to visit from the University of North Carolina. He had promised after the election in 1844 to make such a visit to his alma mater, but the trip had been deferred until the spring of 1847. Polk's acceptance caused the trustees to scurry around to refurbish some of the campus buildings. The college buildings were repainted and Gerrard Hall was enlarged. The trustees had been advised that the president would be accompanied by his wife Sarah and John Mason, secretary of the navy, and his wife. Also in the party were Johanna Rucker, Sarah's niece, Knox Walker, Matthew Fontaine Maury of the navy, and the servants, Elias and Dicey.[45]

In Chapel Hill the president's party was met by William Mercer and Professor Greene, a classmate of Polk, and a delegation of students from the university who were to serve as escorts on the campus. The visitors were also accompanied by many other ladies and gentlemen. At lunchtime the party stopped at Morings, eight miles from Chapel Hill, for lunch. They were joined by John Motley Morehead, ex-governor of North Carolina, and others. At about 6 P.M. the group arrived at Chapel Hill, where they were met by a large group of faculty and students. After a brief stay at the hotel the Polks went to the university chapel where a crowd was gathered. Polk was greeted by D. Y. Swain, the president of the university, who introduced President Polk to the assembled audience.

Sarah and James dined with President Swain and then visited Professor Greene's family. Afterward James took Sarah on a tour of the library and the room he had occupied while a student at the university. The following day was Commencement Day and Polk delivered the baccalaureate sermon. Late that afternoon they set out on their return journey to Washington.[46]

In June 1847 the fiery Jesse Benton Fremont, wife of Lieutenant Colonel John Fremont, visited the Polks. With Mrs. Fremont was Kit Carson, renowned Indian fighter. Kit had accompanied Colonel Fremont as a guide on an exploring expedition to northern California. There were discussions concerning California at that meeting and the president sent messages by Carson to Fremont, who still remained in California.[47]

During that summer, the Polks, with a retinue of staff, officers, and friends, made a tour of the northern and eastern states. There was a grand reception in New York City where people turned out in great numbers. Sarah stayed with the presidential following until it reached Baltimore, where she departed under the protection of Mr. Sumner, a young man from Tennessee who was going home on vacation. Some of Sarah's friends begged her to remain on the tour, but she asked, "Do you want the trouble of having me all through the trip when a separate committee and a separate suite of apartments for my use are always necessary? I could not go with Mr. Polk at the receptions for he was always with the officials, and I could not stand for him to shake hands with the multitude who crowded to see him, the populous, the working man, the high and low whom he must receive."[48]

Today opinions and manners are quite different. Wives accompany gentlemen to all places and assemblies. But in Polk's day it was not thought suitable or dignified for wives to be so prominent or conspicuous.

Sarah's visit to Murfreesboro lasted a week. She went to Nashville to see how the work on their retirement home was coming along. She took numerous measurements and drew a floor plan of the house for reference in furnishing the house. During her stay in Tennessee she had visits with her mother, Elizabeth Childress, and her mother-in-law, Jane Knox Polk. Both Sarah and James were eager for the presidential term to end. Not the least cause for their eagerness was Polk's failing health. They had bought the fine old mansion called Grundy Place. Sarah intended to buy draperies, rugs, and furniture in New York and have them shipped to Nashville in time to have the house furnished for the Polks' retirement.[49]

While in Murfreesboro Sarah received a letter from James dated July 4, 1847:

> *My dear wife,*
> *After I wrote to you at Lowell on the morning of the second instance I proceeded to this place where I was handsomely received and proceeded the same evening to Augusta (the seat of the government of the state), and arrived about one o'clock on the third, found the capitol and the whole city illuminated. On the third (yesterday) I had perhaps as gratifying reception as I have received on my tour. I was received by both branches of the legislature in the hall of the House of Representatives, and was addressed by the governor to which I responded as I think in one of my happiest efforts. Afterwards I was introduced to many of the immense crowd. I can give you no more details, but content myself by saying that my whole visit has been of the most gratifying character. The reception given me by the legislatures and executives of New Hampshire and Maine in their official character as such were highly honorable to me, and were all that my friends could have desired. Nothing of a party or of an unpleasant character has occurred anywhere. I reached here at about midnight last night, and have spent a very quiet day, having been twice to church. Mr. Nathan Clifford, Judge Levi Woodbury, Governor Henry Hubbard, and General Anderson besides many members of Congress with whom I have served have been with me for several days. In a word I am highly delighted with my visit. On tomorrow I proceed on my return. Arriving at Portsmouth, Judge Woodbury's residence. Expect to reach Boston at 5 P.M. and proceed immediately to New York. I will arrive in Washington on Wednesday morning. My health has been good, but my fatigue has been so great that I have been at times almost worn down, and hence some of the newspapers have represented me to be in bad health.*
> *Mr. Burke tells me he has written you today. I will send you several newspapers which will furnish you with many incidents connected with my tour, which I have not time or opportunity to write. I have received no letter from you, except the one you wrote at Wheeling. I hope you reached the end of your journey safely, and I calculate that you are tonight with your mother and sister at Murfreesboro.*
> *Your affectionate husband, James K. Polk*[50]

Secretary of the Navy George Bancroft, who was a great admirer of Sarah Polk, added a postscript to James's letter:

> *P.S. I cannot omit this opportunity of presenting my kindest regards. There was nothing wanting to make our party everything it ought to have been, but your presence. We have got along as well as could be*

expected in your absence. The President has everywhere been received with enthusiasm and has played Republican in grand style. He has made a decided impression on New England. One of the prettiest exhibitions on both sides I have ever witnessed came off last evening between him and Mr. Evans of Maine. The speeches of both were excellent, but I think the President's impromptu reply surpassed the studied effort of the ex-Senator, who has behaved himself exceedingly well throughout.

George Bancroft[51]

It is remarkable that most of the correspondence directed to Sarah came from men. She apparently charmed the menfolk so well that they frequently confided to her their private affairs. As time went by, Bancroft grew to admire Sarah more and more and finally even wrote poetry in her honor.

Chapter 7

Sarah had traveled to Tennessee for the purpose of seeing family and old friends, but she was there also to take care of the business concerned with the renovations of their retirement home. The Polks had acquired Grundy Place, the former home of Judge Felix Grundy, an old friend of the Polks and of Andrew Jackson. Their future home was receiving alterations under the supervision of Vernon Stevenson and others. In October 1847 a powder magazine west of Capitol Hill in Nashville was hit by lightning and a great explosion rocked the area. The walls on the north and west side of the Grundy mansion were so badly damaged that they had to be rebuilt.[1]

During 1847 the Polks suffered from a series of illnesses. In February James was afflicted with a severe cold for several days, and during the months of April, May, and August he had some minor problems also. During September 1847 he had a severe illness, which lasted for two weeks. This illness, with chills and fever occurring at 48-hour intervals, was almost certainly malaria. He had taken home remedies for his first bout, but for the second he summoned two physicians. On Sunday, September 22, 1847, Polk noted in his diary: "I felt too ill to go to church and Mrs. Polk and Colonel and Mrs. Walker (James H.) attended Trinity Church to hear Bishop Otey." On Monday, September 27, he wrote: "I went to my office at the usual hour this morning about 10 A.M. I discovered that I was taking a chill. It continued upon me for two or three hours and was succeeded by considerable fever. I sent for Dr. Hall, who called and prescribed for me about 2 P.M. I requested him to invite Dr. Miller to call with him in the evening. I retired to my room and took the medicine which Dr. Hall had prescribed. In the evening, both Doctors Hall and Miller called, and I spent a restless night.[2]

During four days he had irregular chills and fever, so it is hard to put a more precise label on this type of malaria. Since he recovered in four days, it seems that he must have had quinine prescribed. By

Sunday, October 3 he was free of chills and fever but was so feeble that he had to spend the day in bed.

On Thursday, October 7, Polk noted in his diary that the weather continued to be damp all day. "And I remained all day in my chamber — Mrs. Polk was unwell this evening and I think she had a slight chill. "

On Friday, October 8, Polk noted: "I remained the greater part of the day in my chambers having walked to the office three times and remained there for a short time. I felt much better than I had done since I was taken unwell. ... Mrs. Polk was taken ill yesterday afternoon, continued to be unwell today. She rested on the sofa and sat up throughout the day. She was unwilling to send for physician hoping that the indisposition might pass off. She did not pass a comfortable night."

On Saturday, October 9, he wrote as follows:

> *Mrs. Polk had another chill this A.M. and I sent for Dr. Miller who prescribed for her. Her chill was followed by high fever.*
> *I met with the Cabinet in my office today . On returning to my chamber I found Mrs. Polk quite sick, and with fever. She may have a severe attack.*

On Sunday, October 10, 1847:

> *I spent this day in my chambers until about 4 o'clock P.M. — I am very weak from my late attack, and felt fatigued on my return from my ride. Mrs. Polk was no better. She had another chill and suffered much and rested badly throughout the day and night. Our physician, Dr. Miller, called several times in the course of the day and after night and prescribed for her. She is very nervous and restless, had fever in the latter part of the day, and I thought her very ill.[3]*

Sarah continued quite ill until Wednesday, October 13, when she was declared to be much better and on October 14 Polk noted Sarah was decidedly better. The Polks must have indeed been quite ill during this interval since on Sunday, October 17 they were noted to be insufficiently recovered to go the church.[4]

Polk, punctilious and overly conscientious, seemed almost to apologize to the public for being ill when he noted: "I concluded that if no person had called in that time (referring to his period of illness) who had more important business than those who called today that the public had lost nothing by my absence from the office."[5]

James Polk's utter devotion to long working hours may have contributed to the severe bouts of malaria suffered by him and Sarah. In Polk's time Washington was deserted by the politicians and the affluent during the warm season, when they fled to the mountains and the seashore to escape the heat. The south side of the president's mansion overlooked the Potomac and a canal laden with malaria-carrying mosquitoes. Quinine was available, but there was a high incidence of malaria among those who stayed in the capital in the hot season and exposed themselves to infection.

In August 1847 the White House had been full of visiting relatives, including William Polk and his wife, Samuel Walker, Jane Barnett, Polk's niece, and her husband, Marshall Polk. Polk sent Marshall to a school in Georgetown to try and improve on the poor academic record he had acquired at Georgetown College. Marshall was apparently lazy and had neglected his school work. James confided in Sarah that if Marshall did not do better in his new school, he would be sent home to his mother.[6]

It would be difficult from all available evidence to label Sarah Polk as a snob, but there were occasions when she revealed her belief that people did occupy different strata in the world around her. There is a story about a schoolteacher and her pupils who visited the White House. The schoolmarm engaged Mrs. Polk in a conversation, saying to Sarah that this was the first time she had ever visited the White House. Sarah later said that she was not surprised at the omission, because, though the visiting lady was a woman of culture and of high character, her occupation of schoolteacher barred her from social equality.

Sarah was not greatly interested in the women's rights movement, but she did approve of the movement of women to improve their position in the working world.[7] Were Sarah living today she would doubtless be regarded as a feminist, but in no age could she have been labeled as an overt feminist. If Sarah was concerned with feminism or thought much about it, one cannot determine it from available evidence. She was first lady in July 1848 when Lucretia Mott and Elizabeth Cady Stanton led the first women's rights convention. Mott was a pious Quaker from Philadelphia. Stanton was younger than Mott, but she was more outspoken in her beliefs. Many women gathered at Seneca Falls, a small up-state New York town, to express their aspirations for better education, better job opportunities, more voice in how their children would be raised, and the right to vote.

Although Sarah did not attend the convention, it has been suggested that she urged James to go and address the group. It may be that Sarah, though a feminist at heart, did not attend for fear of ridicule. She did not fully escape the mold imposed by the mores of her time. Her father consciously or unconsciously made an attempt to help Sarah escape certain restrictions imposed on women by seeing that his daughters were well educated.

Sarah had perhaps heard that some individual had expressed the opinion that childless women, such as Sarah, who had little to keep them busy, became involved in affairs beyond their abilities. A Tennessean who wrote to Martin Van Buren could have had the first lady in mind when he wrote something to that effect: "These women, you know, who do not breed must always be busy either in making matches or making and un-making statements or some such things."[8]

The summer of 1848 was spent by Sarah in pursuits that had little connection with feminism, such as renovating their mansion in Nashville. The portraits made of Sarah during her husband's presidency would lend nothing to any contention that she was a feminist. She dressed in elaborate low-cut dresses and her hair styling was very attractive. The women who met at Seneca Falls advocated less elaborate dress and simple hair styling.[9]

With the conclusion of the Mexican War in May 1848, the pressure on both James and Sarah lessened. Yet even after the trip to Fortress Monroe for a so-called vacation, the president's health was so poor that he was compelled to seek refuge in spas in Virginia and Pennsylvania. From the White House where she was detained by the usual guests, relatives, and others, Sarah wrote:

> *Dear Husband, I do hope that when you receive this note you will not say to yourself that your wife is as annoying as the office seekers persecuting you wherever you go by compelling you to open and read a little budget of nonsense of my own sad complaints that I am separated from you. Yesterday, not being very well, I kept to my room and felt disconsolate, everything bore the appearance of universal quietness. The doorbell rang only a few times. I beg you to stay long enough in Bedford to renovate your health. Grieved as I might be at your absence (don't think I am jesting) I do not wish you to leave there before Monday week; a shorter time cannot benefit. How often do you intend to write me?[10]*

In this, and in about every letter Sarah wrote to James, there was a note of endearment and one of solicitude for his health. When Polk was at Bedford, Pennsylvania, he received another letter from his wife:

> *Dear Husband, I am this morning distressed on your account at the change of the weather, fearing that you will be discouraged and will return home without benefit to yourself. I hope that you will not get sick, and know that you will keep a large fire, and wish that you would stay as long as you intended when you left. There is nothing to call your attention back here so soon. I saw Mr. Buchanan last evening; he was full of foreign news; but I learned nothing very specific. I did not go to church on yesterday. I coughed so much I was afraid of disturbing the congregation. I would be very happy to be with you today at Bedford. The visit of our family circle to Mount Vernon has passed off very well. A visit to New York and Tennessee is still on the tapis and when they will be accomplished is more than I can tell. I heard from you verbally on yesterday morning. I fear that you will be taken up with the democracy of Pennsylvania, that you will not find time to write me. If it rains tomorrow as it does today I will look for you back on Wednesday. Not that I think you ought to come, but knowing you as well as I do, I fear that you will. I beg you to be patient and wait for sunshine. Sarah*[11]

Polk and his diary noted on February 4, 1849, that Henry Clay had called at the White House. Polk met the failed Whig candidate in the parlor below the stairs. The president stated that he received his bitter political antagonist with all the politeness he could summon.

Clay told Polk that he had been in the capital for several weeks visiting with friends, and apologized for not calling before. Clay said that he entertained no feelings toward Polk of an unkind character. Polk responded that he too held no feeling of enmity. At that moment, Sarah came in the parlor and Clay continued the pleasant conversation with her. As he was leaving, he remarked to Sarah in a very pleasant manner that he would visit her drawing rooms soon, and that he had heard a great deal of approbation concerning her administration, but he believed that there was some difference in opinion about her husband's administration. Sarah replied pleasantly that she was glad to hear from him that her administration was approved and added, "If a political opponent of my husband is to succeed him I have always said that I prefer you, Mr. Clay, and in that event I shall be glad to surrender the White House to you." Clay left the White House in an excellent humor.[12]

There were those other than Sarah who were aware of Polk's waning strength. The Mexican War had imposed great burdens and cares
on the president. Charles Ingersoll, while visiting Sarah, told her that
the president was wearing himself out with constant and excessive work
and that if he did not take some recreation he would die soon after the
close of his term. The congressman strongly advised that Sarah take
the president on carriage rides morning and evening to get time away
from his cares. However, the Polks seldom went out on the prescribed
carriage rides, for someone was always in the office, and James would
not or could not come out.[13]

Throughout Polk's presidency, many relatives of both James and
Sarah visited the White House. Some of them had such prolonged stays
that they seemed to have taken up permanent residence. Polk's diary
records the visits of nephews, nieces, cousins, a brother, sisters, and
various in-laws. Some of these visits came at times when the Polks were
least able, on account of their state affairs, to receive them. There was,
however, never an instance when James and Sarah seemed to be less
than cordial to any guest. Their welcoming of young persons may
have had something to do with the fact that they were childless. For
most of the entertainment of these relatives, James leaned heavily on
Sarah.

Their personal involvement with their young visitors demonstrated
the very human side of the Polks. An extended stay was enjoyed first
by a niece, Johanna Rucker of Murfreesboro, the daughter of Sarah's
sister Susan. Johanna arrived in the capital of October 1845 and remained
for almost two years. She finally left the White House in June 1847 to
go with her aunt Sarah on a trip to Tennessee. Following Johanna, no
niece remained at the president's mansion for any prolonged period of
time until the fall of 1848. Then Sarah Polk Rucker (Johanna's sister),
Virginia Hayes (the daughter of Ophelia), and Polk's sister (Clarissa
Polk Hayes) lived at the White House as visitors until the end of the
president's term in March 1849.[14]

There were other visitors, however, who were a source of considerable concern to James and Sarah. None created more of a problem
and took more of their precious time than James's nephew, Marshall
Polk. Marshall, who at age 14 showed some of the immaturity found
in James's brother William, was the son of Marshall Tate Polk, who
was deceased. Perhaps it was the boy's frail health that led Polk to take
such interest in the lad when he assumed the role of a father.[15]

In early 1845 Marshall had accepted the president's offer to send him to Georgetown College. When the offer came, the young man answered, "I will go cheerfully and beg that you will forget the reluctance I have shown in doing that which you thought best for me. I promise that in the future I will exert myself all that I can to advance myself in my studies with as little expense [sic] as possible, and as little trouble to you."[16] The president's experience with Marshall was full of promises that were not to be fulfilled. Perhaps James's experience with William, his younger brother, had given him some idea in how to deal with a teenager who did not easily adapt himself to academic life.[17]

Polk was not one to give up on brothers or nephews; he enrolled Marshall at Georgetown College and paid for all of his expenses. Marshall finished his second year at Georgetown, but his academic standing at the end of two years was so poor that the president withdrew the young man and placed him in another school, also in Georgetown, run by two ministers: the Reverend Whittington and the Reverend Spencer. The young man performed scholastically no better with the reverends than he had at Georgetown, so his disappointed uncle moved him to yet a third school, in Alexandria, which was run by Benjamin Hallowell. In the spring of 1848 Polk arranged for Marshall to be enrolled at the U.S. Military Academy, but to the president's disappointment the young man was in trouble at the academy from the time he was enrolled. Marshall's poor record at West Point was due not only to poor academics but also poor conduct.[18]

Polk perhaps would have never been a faithful attendee of Sunday's worship had it not been for Sarah. He became, due to her encouragement, a regular occupant of a pew in the First Presbyterian Church. It is a tribute to Sarah's power of persuasion that of the 183 Sundays noted in Polk's diary he was in church 147 of them. This is indeed a phenomenal record of church attendance for a president. In 1846 Polk missed only six Sundays during the year. Sickness and bad weather were responsible for five absences during 1847 and 1848, and there were some occasions when the affairs of state kept him from attending.[19]

Although James was a regular churchgoer and entertained some of the same Calvinist beliefs that Sarah held, he resisted throughout his life any attempt to affiliate directly with the church of Calvin and Knox. It is strange and confusing that he, raised in a home where his mother was a strong Presbyterian, should become interested in

Methodism. During his congressional campaigns, he had attended a Methodist camp meeting. Perhaps he yearned for the warmth and assurances delivered by that evangelist. Although James attended the Presbyterian church regularly during his presidency — perhaps to please Sarah — he preferred the Methodist church.[20]

On March 3, 1848, the day ending the third year as president, he grumbled that his three years as president had been years of incessant labor, anxiety, and responsibility. A year earlier Polk had reflected, "In truth though I occupy a very high position I am the hardest working man in this country." In September 1847, on Sarah's birthday, Polk failed to mention the occasion; instead he complained about the heavy burden of his office: "With me it is emphatically true that the presidency is no bed of roses."[21]

Throughout May and early June 1848 Polk was again ill with malaria and was treated by Doctors Hall and Miller. In spite of his depleted strength, he continued to attend to his duties. In June he had the added problem of chronic diarrhea. Sarah was very concerned about his illness and worried over him constantly.

July 14, 1848, was the date scheduled for the ceremony for laying the cornerstone of the Washington Monument and, characteristically, Polk — in spite of his poor health — attended the ceremony. James rode on horseback and was saluted by the military who lined Pennsylvania Avenue.[22]

As Polk's retirement neared, Sarah continued to grace the White House as hostess, able administrator, and strong supporter of her husband's views. In the latter part of Polk's term the crusty old Charles Sumner, senator from Massachusetts whose political views were almost diametrically opposed to those of Polk, said, "Sarah's sweetness of manner won me entirely."[23]

By 1849 the use of gas lighting was in general use in public places, but was not yet used much in dwellings. When the installation work began at the White House, Sarah was adamant that the reception room with the elegant chandeliers should remain unchanged and continued to be lit with wax candles. It was announced that the next reception at the White House would be lit with gas. However, after the expectant guests arrived, the gas supply failed and the brilliant lights went out, leaving the White House in darkness save for the reception room, which was well lit with its wax candles.[24]

James was one who believed in observing anniversaries. He observed on February 13, 1849, that exactly four years earlier he had arrived in the capital as president-elect. He repeated that the four years had been full of hard work and heavy responsibility, but he also expressed excitement and a feeling of profound relief that he would now be able to pass the burden on to the next president. He declared, "I will soon cease to be a servant and will become a sovereign." He was anxious for the day when, "As a private citizen I will have no one but myself to serve and will exercise a part of the sovereign power of my country."[25]

It is certain that Polk, in February 1849 as well as when he became president, realized that he could not physically survive a second term. From a thorough review of Polk's health history, it is obvious that the reason he had declared he would not run for a second term was as much physical as political. If he had not had Sarah to lean upon, it is probable that he would not have endured a single full term in the White House. Sarah, who had been at his side night and day, watched him decline with growing anxiety, and she expressed profound relief that they could shed the great responsibilities and return to Tennessee.

The *Ladies National Magazine* in March 1849 carried a tribute to Sarah written by the renowned poet, Anne Stephen. The third stanza of this widely read and copied poem reads as follows:

> There, standing in our nation's home
> My memory ever pictures thee,
> As some bright dome of ancient Rome,
> Modest yet all a queen should be
> I love to keep thee in my mind,
> Thus mated with the pure of old,
> When love with lofty deeds combine,
> Made woman great and warriors bold.[26]

The *Washington Post* also saluted Sarah with a poem at the time of her departure. The author is unknown:

> A Farewell to Mrs. Polk
> Lady, farewell! amid the gloom of grief
> How many a heart will utter that sad sound.
> Farewell! for a thousand hearts will mourn,
> So much of friendship lost, of sorrow found.
> And thou wilt leave a void in friendship's hall.
> Where joyous notes were once so wont to rise,

Like that fair pleiad which forsook its home,
And caused to mourn the sisters of the skies.
But thou must go; yet with these thou shalt bear
A stranger's hope upon the distant way,
And only fade to give a calmer day.
A welcome, too, I'd give thee to my home,
My sunny home, the old Palmetto soil.
Where many a heart, all warm and true and kind,
Shall chase away the gloom of travels toil,
And may life pass as soft as sunset hour,
When gentle rays gleam on the skies above,
And may each pulse in sweetest union beat,
To the soft music of the harp of love.[27]

It is not strange that Sarah received so many warm accolades. She had a uniqueness that drew people to her and caused them to praise her and confide in her. Her personality had a great effect on James's cold and humorless state. One writer undertook the labor of writing a book on presidential wit. He devoted 23 three pages to Lyndon Johnson and half a page to James Polk. Of the two anecdotes attributed to Polk, one was concerned with office seekers and the other with the method of shaking hands. Perhaps the most witty thing in the section on Polk's wit was that the writer introduced him as a Whig, which must have made Polk turn in his grave.[28]

On Thursday, March 1, James and Sarah held their final dinner party in honor of president-elect Zachary Taylor. Polk had invited many members of both his own party and that of the Whigs. The president-elect and the defeated Cass were seated on either side of Sarah. Senator John Bell, Polk's old political rival, and Representative Jefferson Davis were paired because there were not enough ladies present to give each man a partner.

After the party was over and the guests had gone, Sarah told James that she thought it was the most pleasant of all their White House dinners. James responded, "Yes, it was a friendly tranquil evening. I wish we were leaving tomorrow."[29]

Two days after Polk and Sarah had hosted their last White House party, they began to prepare to vacate the presidential mansion. On the same day the cabinet members came to formally submit their resignations. Polk wrote in his diary: "I am disposed of all the business on my table down to the minutest detail, and at the close of the day left a clean table for my successor."

At sunset on March 3 Polk surveyed his office for the last time, and went with Sarah and two nieces to a hotel where they were to remain for the next few days.

Polk was not very happy with his successor, General Zachary Taylor, and before Polk retired he noted his final impression of his successor.

"General Taylor is, I have no doubt, a well-meaning man. He is, however, uneducated, exceedingly ignorant of public affairs, and I should judge of very ordinary capacity. He will be in the hands of others, and may rely wholly upon his cabinet to administer the government."[30]

Sarah and James went to church for the last time and occupied their customary pews. Their pastor, Rev. E. Ballentine, delivered the sermon. At the end of the service the minister and members of the congregation approached the president and his wife with expressions of their friendship and affectionate regards.[31]

James and Sarah departed from Washington on March 6 for Tennessee. At the time of the ex-president's departure he had a severe cold and was exhausted by the stress and hard work of his last few weeks in office. He was in great need of a prolonged period of relaxation, but such was not to be. The Polks had been persuaded, by public demand, to make their way home by a circuitous, southern route. A very intensive schedule of entertainment and celebration had been prepared to greet them. Accompanied from one city to the next by committees, Polk was not allowed any repose. His homeward pilgrimage took him through Virginia, North and South Carolina, and Georgia. The train trip across Georgia was hot and dusty, and the carriages were drenched by heavy rain as they passed through Alabama. The Polks rode in a closed carriage, but gusty winds came through cracks. The travelers were cold, wet, and uncomfortable. When they reached Montgomery, Alabama, Polk's cold had greatly worsened. He suffered from a harassing cough, headache, and an exaggeration of his chronic diarrhea. His tour through the South had now become a test of sheer endurance.[32]

Sarah wrote a letter to her mother from Columbus, Georgia:

> At Petersburg, as everywhere else, we were greeted with great cordiality. Whitefield's Hotel and other buildings were illuminated in our honor. On Wednesday we arrived in Wilmington. Bells were rung and we were met by a large crowd of people who escorted us to Swann's

Hotel. The military entertained us with stirring music. Jim and I received many callers throughout the day. Mr. Arthur Hill, an old college classmate of Jim's called. They had not seen each other since their graduation thirty years before. We were also met by an advance welcome committee from Charleston. We left Wilmington Thursday morning at ten o'clock on the steamer Governor Dudley. A crowd was assembled and parting salutes were given us by artillery. The boat stopped at Smithwell for about two hours where we viewed an old block house of the revolutionary period. It was identified with the first assertion of independence. Many pressed to pay their respects to us. Friday, we landed [at] Gadsden's Wharf in Charleston, South Carolina. The ladies and I were escorted by a special welcome committee to the Carolina Hotel where apartments had been prepared for us. Mr. W. H. O'Connor offered us the hospitality of the city. He was also a fellow student with Jim at Chapel Hill.

Jim was escorted in an open carriage parade by citizens and the military. The reception was brilliant, orderly, and in very good taste. We later drove to Saint Andrew's Hotel with the city authorities and many citizens. I can hardly believe that when we left Washington there was snow and ice, for the weather here is unseasonably warm. The sudden transition from cold to hot has given Jim a terrible cold and he is much fatigued. Early the next morning our party was taken in an open carriage to board the steamboat for Savannah, Georgia. Governor Seabrook accompanied us for as far as Beaufort, South Carolina. None of us were seasick for the weather was calm and the sea was very smooth. Our vessel was sighted from the bluff above Savannah at about nine that evening, and the town was notified by signal rockets. Guns saluted us as the boat approached the landing. When we reached the wharf, the mayor accompanied by quite a few citizens was introduced to us. After that we went to Pulaski House where James received visits from citizens at the Armory Hall. The next day being Sunday, we attended the Independent Presbyterian Church in the company of the mayor. An unusual thing happened as we sat down. People began passing us hymn books and with every book there was a bouquet of violets, roses, or some other fragrant flower. We took the flowers, appreciating the compliment, and returned the song books, for we could use but one. Jim also attended an Episcopal church that afternoon with the mayor. Early Monday morning we took the train to Macon, Georgia. People were collected all the way to greet us. We spent the night at the Floyd House. On Tuesday, there were many speeches and receptions in our honor. Jim made a speech and as usual it was beautifully delivered. His manner is always so quiet, calm and dignified, yet clear and commanding. I always just love hearing his voice, for it is so soft and melodious.

That night Sarah and Virginia attended a ball in our honor. Jim was just too worn out to go. I am very concerned that Jim is pushing himself too hard. It will be a relief to get home and rest.

We left Macon early the next morning and occupied a coach with just the family, which was restful, although the girls chattered incessantly about the previous night's ball. In the afternoon there was a violent thunderstorm with heavy rain which impeded our progress a great deal. We were entertained at Forsyth, Barnsville, and Thomaston. By dark we still had many miles to go to reach Columbus. Another thunderstorm more violent than that of the afternoon struck us. It was accompanied by heavy rain and even some hail. The driver could not control the frightened horses, so we stopped the coach. Henry and Elias had to hold the horses 'til the storm abated. So we didn't arrive until 9 P.M. We are staying at General Lowe's.

I will tell you about the rest of the journey when I arrive there. I am so anxious to see all of my friends and relatives and be home again.[33]

Polk and Sarah had visualized a river trip on the *Emperor* to Mobile as two days of rest, peace, and quiet. Such was not to be. At every landing there was a throng of Polk admirers waiting to come on board and greet the retiring president and his wife. The Polks, just after their boarding, were accosted by a backwoods parson, who persuaded them to sit through a two-hour service in the ornate ladies' cabin. The preacher struck them as unusually ignorant, but his sincerity touched the Polks.

Sarah, as the boat resumed its way down the river, said, "Poor man, he was even less well-off than the people he was trying to help. Imagine owning nothing but the clothes on your back. I gave him a five dollar gold piece."[34]

That night a passenger died, presumably of cholera. The victim was buried on the bank of the river. The Polks had learned at Montgomery that there was a recurrence of a cholera epidemic in New Orleans. The Polks were alarmed, but they had gone too far to turn back.[35]

Their concerns were justified, for in 1849 Asiatic cholera was present in epidemic proportions throughout the Mississippi Valley.

Cholera is an acute illness caused by bacteria (vibrio cholerae) that infects the small intestine. It is characterized by massive diarrhea, rapid dehydration, and electrolyte depletion. Death rates run as high as 60 percent where there is no effective treatment.

After the *Emperor* arrived in Mobile, it was met by two steamers full of passengers who desired to greet the Polks. The two boats were lashed on each side of the *Emperor*. The committee from Mobile came on board first, followed soon thereafter by many ladies and gentlemen who crowded onto the steamer. Polk, at the request of the committee, boarded both boats, where he shook hands with many people. Afterward he returned to the *Emperor* and joined Sarah where she was receiving ladies.[36]

On Thursday, March 20, 1849, James noted in his diary:

> *I rose this morning much exhausted from my fatigue and the excessively warm weather for this time of year, even in this climate. In addition to this I was still somewhat indisposed.*
>
> *From the moment breakfast was over I was occupied in receiving visitors. The cholera I learned was prevailing to some extent in Mobile but was not epidemic. I consulted Dr. Knotts, an eminent physician of the place, who prescribed for me and gave me medicine to be used in case of an attack of cholera of my party. He informed me that the disease was prevailing in New Orleans and advised me in my state of health to spend as little time as possible in that city, and I resolved that when I reached that city I would take the first boat bound for Nashville. About one o'clock we left the hotel. I was conveyed in an open carriage to the boat bound for New Orleans, escorted by the committee, authorities of the city, and a crowd of persons in the street. The boat left the wharf between one and two o'clock. We had a smooth sea and a pleasant afternoon though unusually warm for the season. Colonel Watson and two other members of the Montgomery Committee continued to accompany me. Nothing of interest occurred during the afternoon and night. I was relieved by having some opportunity to rest.*[37]

Dr. Knotts told Sarah, "You can insist on leaving immediately, but your husband cannot do so without seeming to undervalue the honors the city has been arranging for him." James did attend a dinner, but he withdrew early in response to Sarah's pleas. The throng of persons wishing to greet the Polks was so large that James was obliged to greet them in one parlor and Sarah in another. Sarah was so concerned about her husband's welfare that she tried to coax him into leaving immediately. She said, "Let's bear the rest of the expense so we can be free to go straight home from here." The expenses for the trip had been borne by the different committees along the route of travel. Sarah continued, "The committee told me that a steamer would carry us to Nashville without charge, but it won't be ready until the day set by our original plans and I want to go now." James answered, "You are right my dear. There is a commercial steamer leaving for Nashville tomorrow, and I have already booked a passage in it." Sarah was pleased by this news and left immediately to tell Knotts to cancel the rest of the itinerary.[38]

Chapter 8

The political lives of the Polks were over. It was natural that the former president should make every effort to see that his niche in history was preserved. James Polk reveled in the plaudits of the masses who came to meet him along the way from the capital to New Orleans. That he endured the pressures of long days and endless handshaking when he was very ill is quite remarkable. That he did so showed his great desire to be remembered favorably by the people. The Polks' premature departure from New Orleans proves that he was very ill at the time, very ill indeed. Nothing else would have persuaded a politician — candidate or retired — to depart a stage where he was receiving continuous applause. It is doubtful if Polk would have left even then, had it not have been for the urging of Sarah.

Departing from New Orleans on one of the regularly scheduled trips of the *Colonel E. Watkins*, James and Sarah left the boat only twice on their run up the Mississippi. The final time was at Baton Rouge, where he spent an hour with friends but was too ill and exhausted to accept any invitations. James was in a state of near collapse. His problems with diarrhea had remained quite severe and depleting.

The word that the president and his wife were on board the *Watkins* had reached several ports of call along the way. At each stop huge crowds clamored for a look at the retired president. His faithful servant Elias helped him dress and go on deck for a brief moment to receive the cheers of the crowd. At other times he remained in bed too ill to eat, sleep, or rest. He was actually too weak to walk without support.[1]

At that time there was only the unchecked debilitating diarrhea and none of the severe symptoms associated with cholera, such as abdominal pain, severe thirst, and vomiting. James and Sarah were further alarmed to learn that one of the passengers had died on the first day out of New Orleans, and on the second day that three other passengers were in late, severe stages of cholera.[2] On March 24, 1849, Polk wrote in his diary: "By ten o'clock this morning we reached

Natchez, Mississippi. Our approach was announced by the firing of cannons on the shore. The boat touched the shore where a large number of people were assembled. I was suffering so much from my excessive fatigue and was so much indisposed that I decided not to go on shore — I regretted the necessity which my health imposed on me to decline the proffered honor."[3]

Again on March 28 Polk noted in his diary that when the boat reached Paducah, he sent on shore for a physician. A Dr. Jones came on board to examine Polk. He determined that it was not cholera, but since all diseases of the bowel had a tendency to run into cholera when that disease was prevalent, he advised James to leave the boat. Polk requested that the doctor travel with him on the boat to Smithland. Dr. Jones agreed to do so and after going ashore for medicine he accompanied Polk to Smithland. Polk was administered an unspecified medicine, and upon arrival at Smithland he and Sarah left the boat and went to a hotel. When James arrived at his room, he sent for a Dr. Saunders, who after examination came to the same conclusion as Dr. Jones. Polk learned from his physician that cholera was present with high mortality on all the boats coming up from New Orleans.[4] Polk's illness detained the presidential party at Smithland for several days until he improved They arrived in Nashville later than expected.[5]

On April 3, 1849, the *Nashville Union* reported as follows:

> The reception of Mr. Polk yesterday, although entirely spontaneous, was one of the most enthusiastic ever witnessed. He was expected last Friday and arrangements for his receptions were interrupted by news of his sickness at Smithland. Most intense anxiety for his health has pervaded the city, which was relieved by the intelligence yesterday morning that he would be in Nashville Monday morning. By 11:00 the steamboat landing was crowded. The steamer arrived at our wharf about 12:00, and Mr. Polk was escorted by the multitude to the courthouse square, where he was addressed by the governor, Neill S. Brown, in an eloquent speech. The feebleness of the late president was apparent, and it was scarcely expected he would do more than make an acknowledgment of the reception. But he seemed to be inspired from the moment of the first word which fell from his lips to forget his feebleness and to renew his ancient energy. His speech was touching, and he referred in eloquent terms to the happiness of reaching home. At the conclusion of the ceremony Mr. Polk was escorted to the veranda where he and his wife were visited by a large number of citizens.[6]

The Polks spent the next day in Nashville, and James left his hotel room only to make occasional visits to the hotel parlor to converse with an old friend. On the afternoon of April 3 James and Sarah went in their carriage to look at their retirement home, Polk Place, which was not yet finished. Sarah had earlier visited the place and had done most of the planning. Returning to their hotel, James and Sarah retired to their room. They planned to go on the next day to visit James's mother and some of his relatives at Columbia.

In his diary on April 4 James wrote as follows:

> *This morning, though still feeble, I rode out with Mrs. Polk in a private carriage to pay a visit to my mother and other relatives and friends at my old residence at Columbia. We dined at Franklin where a number of people called to see me. They had not been advised that I would pass Franklin that day and there was no formal reception. After dinner we rode as far as Cartwright's Inn on the road near the village of Spring Hill, where I stopped for the night. Mr. Kelly and Mr. Garth from Columbia met me at Cartwright's. They informed me that there would be a public reception at Columbia on tomorrow.[7]*

Anyone reading about the trip from Washington to Nashville and Polk's illness en route would conclude that Polk, aside from his decision to leave New Orleans early, used extremely poor judgment in his failure to preserve his strength. Any reasonable observer would have judged that from New Orleans to Nashville he should have spent the full time resting rather than receiving visitors. His reserve was so depleted that after he arrived in Nashville he should have gone into seclusion and rested for weeks.

The Polks had to reside a few days at the commercial hotel while their new home was being fitted for occupancy. While waiting, they made visits to Sarah's mother in Murfreesboro and James's mother in Columbia. The Polks were greeted with enthusiasm in both towns. In Columbia James was honored by the citizens of Maury, Marshall, Giles, and Lewis counties. General Pillow, a hero of the Mexican War, made the welcoming address. On their return to Nashville and Polk Place, they found their new home ready, and they celebrated by entertaining many old and new friends.[8]

James was improved somewhat, but he was still far from well. It was noted by those who knew him well that he looked many years older than when he entered the White House. His hair was snow white, his face was lined, and he looked older than his mother.[9]

On April 4, 1849 Polk entered a note in his diary:

> After breakfast this morning having made a visit to Mrs. Polk's rela-
> tives we left Murfreesboro and returned to Nashville, where we arrived
> at 3:00. We stopped at our own home [Polk Place]. The workmen had
> not finished it, but two or three rooms had been fitted up so that we
> could occupy them. Numerous boxes of furniture, books, groceries, and
> other articles forwarded from New York, New Orleans, and Columbia,
> Tennessee, were piled up in the halls and rooms; and the whole estab-
> lishment, except for two or three apartments presented the appearance of
> great disorder and confusion. Our faithful steward, Henry Bowman,
> had in our absence to Columbia and Murfreesboro caused the carpets to
> be made and put down in some of the rooms and caused our furniture
> to be opened. Our servants had arrived from Columbia and were com-
> fortably settled in the servants' house. We thought it best to take posses-
> sion of the house at once and superintend the arrangement necessary to
> put it in order. From this day therefore may be dated our first occupa-
> tion of our new home in Nashville.[10]

The Nashville to which the Polks returned was no longer a frontier town, and the social standards adopted there were imported from
old Virginia and the Carolinas by the leaders of the area. Those visitors who came to Nashville were impressed by the elegance and neat-
ness of the town and the taste displayed in the arrangements of the better residences.

The dress and manners were much the same, but the social roles
had changed. In the older society a man knew his status; in the new
country he assumed it. Lineage counted for little in the west; wealth
counted for much and a gentleman was known by his clothes. A lofty
military bearing was preferred in Nashville, and a pompous pose could
carry a man far. Education was not respected and refinement was often
lacking.[11]

As for the costume of the women, the simple old men who had
grown up on the frontier much objected to the elegance and extravagance of their dress. A Mr. Ludlow observed thus:

> If the old ladies of that day had met with one of our slender, pale-
> faced fashionable belles, rattling in silk and satins — her clothing drawn
> over her delicate limbs as tight as the skin upon a lean weasel — her waist
> belted up in buckram until compressed within the circumference of six

inches — her snow white bosom peeping over the top of her outer garments, protected only by the slight covering of gauze, ribbons, and lace — a monstrous staked and ridered bonnet upon her head, streaming with flounces and furbelows — a green veil, half as long as her whole person, hanging over her face and fluttering its ample folds in the winds as she journeyed onward — a bunch of jewelry, as large as a wagoner's horse bells, suspended from each ear, and dangling upon her shoulders — her dress cut and made according to the fashion of the present day — her delicate ancles [*sic*] covered only by a pair of thin, flesh colored hose, at that day calling stockings, and her tender little trampers encompassed within a pair of prunella slippers, they would have set all the bear dogs upon her.[12]

Stage lines from every direction brought commerce and culture into Nashville. The Nashville Theater presented widely known actors such as Junius Brutus Booth, Edwin Forrest, Edmond Keen, and Tyrone Power. A traveler who was lodging in Nashville Inn compared it favorably to the Tontin Coffee House in New York.[13]

Nashville educational institutions included the famous Nashville Female Academy and the University of Nashville. Thus, when the Polks arrived in 1849, Nashville possessed all of the amenities to be found in a town that had long since lost its frontier flavor. The Polks' Nashville home, their last, was surrounded by a tall, wrought-iron fence and guarded by imposing gates. Stone steps led onto a portico supported by four large columns. The central two columns were fluted; the two lateral columns were square and smooth. On either end of the mansion were large single-storied wings. The main entry from the portico was a central massive doorway leading to a spacious hallway, which opened on the left and right into large parlors. On the east side of the house was another entry from the portico. A similar hallway on the north side connected with the main hallway to lead to the dining room and other rooms. The grounds on the east side sloped gradually to Vine Street; the east gate was made of a huge anchor topped by the American eagle.

In the center of the main hallway stood a round table, topped with Egyptian marble inlaid with a mosaic of colored marble, showing the American eagle, and which bore the coat of arms of the United States. On the outer edge of the marble were 30 white stars representing the states in the union at that time.

The library contained shelves of books extending from floor to ceiling. Above the mantle hung two embroidered addresses by Polk:

one as governor of Tennessee and the other as president of the United States, his first message to Congress. All the lettering on these historic documents was done on white satin, and they were in matching gilt frames.[14]

The Polks seemed well established in their new home. They had overseen the construction and furnishing of their elegant antebellum mansion and now visited their family and friends. Polk arranged and catalogued his vast array of papers, documents, and books. For a few weeks he seemed to gain strength and vigor, but the recovery did not last for long. Polk was still very frail, prematurely aged, and vulnerable to any illness that came his way. During his lifetime he had suffered from several debilitating illnesses. First, in his late teens he had undergone the operation for urinary bladder stones, followed in later years by recurring attacks of malaria and chronic diarrhea. The actual cause of his diarrhea is undetermined since laboratory studies of stools were not available at that time.

In late May 1849 James announced to Sarah that he had heard from one of his nephews, Sam Caldwell, who was staying at a local hotel. The young man had earlier spent several days at Polk Place prior to his departure to travel east on business. However, because of a severe chill, Sam had been unable to catch the stage to Louisville.

The Polks sent Elias to the hotel to tell the young man that he must immediately come to Polk Place. James did not wish to alarm Sarah, but he told her that several deaths had been reported to have occurred in Nashville due to cholera. When Elias returned from the hotel, he reported that Sam was in bed under a doctor's care but was not seriously ill. The next morning James called on his nephew at the hotel; finding him not very ill, he insisted that they return to Polk Place. James called Dr. Rucker to attend Sam, and the Polks nursed the young man through a mild attack of cholera.[15]

On Sunday, June 3, 1849, James had a severe recurrence of diarrhea, accompanied by vomiting. His illness did not respond as it had done previously to opiates. Sarah noted that his face was ashen. The symptoms, coupled with the fact that he had been exposed to cholera in Nashville, led his doctors to assume that he had contracted cholera.[16]

All that the assembled doctors could do was lament the failure of their methods of treatment. Earlier, all of the symptoms had been present, such as vomiting, abdominal cramps, cyanosis, dehydration, and profound weakness. Polk surprisingly survived for several days with symptoms that were usually associated with death in a few hours or days. The symptoms had unexpectedly gone away and he seemed improved; however, there was sudden relapse into the final stage of the disease.

He lingered for a few days, but when Polk realized that he was near death, he called for the Reverend John McFerrin of the McKendree Methodist Church. James wished formal admission into the church through baptism. The baptismal rites were performed by McFerrin. James's mother had traveled from Murfreesboro with her own minister — a Presbyterian — in tow, hoping to persuade James to be baptized and be admitted to her church, but Polk elected to establish this final relationship with Methodism. He lingered until June 15, 1849, when he succumbed to the illness.[17]

At a much earlier date Polk had written in his diary: "Mrs. Polk being a member of the Presbyterian Church, I generally attend that church with her, though my opinion and my predeliction are in favor of the Methodist Church."

Johanna Rucker, his niece, also stated that Methodism was her preference as a church and that she took great pride in being a Methodist. On his fiftieth birthday, November 2, 1845, James had set down some thoughts on his religious beliefs. The preacher the Sunday before had expounded on the topic of Judgment Day. James wrote: "That I had lived fifty years and that before fifty years more would expire I would be sleeping with the generations that had gone before me, I thought of the vanities of this world, how little they would profit me half a century since, and that it was time for me to be putting my house in order."[18]

Polk continued gradually to sink, and at 4:40 P.M. on June 15 he passed away without a struggle, simply ceasing to breathe. He was in his fifty-fourth year. About 30 minutes before his death, his mother entered his room and, kneeling by his bedside, offered up a beautiful prayer and committed her son to the king of kings and lord of lords.[19]

The news of Polk's deathbed acceptance of Christianity and his quandary over which sect should baptize him aroused a great deal of theological controversy. One writer exclaimed, "Well might the dying president be ashamed of his late hour. It was not wise, not safe, not reputable ... thus to put off joining the church." However, one must feel that the deathbed baptismal rites were only a formal recognition of his long-held beliefs. Those who have done extensive study of the lives of the Polks feel that since Sarah was such a firm Presbyterian, Polk did not wish to show any disloyalty to her by becoming a Methodist.[20]

Throughout the terrible ordeal of Polk's last illness, the doctors and all attendants were astonished to see the fortitude and composure shown by Sarah. She had remained in the sickroom day and night and slept on a cot near her husband. Even her meals were served there so she would not have to leave his side. She had not gone from his room at any time for more than a few minutes. In James's presence she maintained an impassive front and continued to express confidence in his recovery.[21]

After James's death Sarah suffered great grief. During their union of 25 years, they had known little separation. Theirs was a togetherness rarely seen in any marriage. Sarah had been at his side always, during long days of work and at repose. They had shared everything. When she lost him, she said, "life was then a blank."[22]

The funeral rites were held on the next day and, in observance of Polk's death, all places of business were closed. The citizens of Nashville showed great respect for their former president; almost everyone in that city followed the funeral train to Polk's last resting place. He was buried dressed in a plain black suit holding a copy of the Constitution of the United States, the document that Polk had adhered to so religiously. The Rev. McFerrin remembered the text he had used at the camp meeting Polk had attended years earlier and used the same text for the funeral rites.[23]

James was first buried in the Nashville City Cemetery, but a year after his death he was removed from the cemetery to Polk Place. Strangely, the tomb and superstructural outline resembled a prophetic piece of needlework that Sarah had saved from her days at the Moravian Female Academy. The piece, which she kept, pictured a white tomb, worked in chenille on a white satin background, which gleamed through the different shades of green, brown, and yellow of the trees.[24] Built of Tennessee white marble, the actual tomb had a double vault and a space for Sarah's own epitaph. When James was finally interred at Polk Place, it was placed in front and to the left of their home. Polk Place and his mausoleum became Nashville's chief visitor attraction.[25]

When Polk died, Sarah was only 45. She was at that time still striking in appearance, financially wealthy, and very intelligent; but she now had to establish a life for herself. James's last will and testament left nearly everything to his wife. Since he was legal guardian of his nephew, Marshall, Polk also made a bequest to him. The substance of the will read as follows: "I have entire confidence that my beloved wife, Sarah Polk, who has constantly been identified with me in all of her sympathies and affections through all of the vicissitudes of my public and private life for more than twenty-five years, and who by her prudence, care, and economy, has aided and assisted me in acquiring and preserving the property which I own, will at her death make a proper and just disposition of what property she may then possess."[26]

Chapter 9

Sarah turned the inside of the Polk mansion into a memorial for her dead husband. James's study was precisely as he had left it. His papers, his books, and his pen were displayed just as he had left them. On the second floor in the great hall was James's library and the letters he had received, filed and labeled in his script.[1]

Sarah was intent on preserving not only her husband's memory but his place in history. She was hostess at Polk Place and curator of what amounted to a James Polk museum. In her husband's will he left the Mississippi cotton plantation to Sarah. Sarah's management of that plantation reveals much about her that was not evidenced elsewhere.

James had always paid top wages to his plantation employees, and since the overseer, Mr. Mairs, had served James well, Sarah raised his pay, hoping that such action would encourage him to continue. She then requested that her overseer report to her each month. For the record, Sarah kept and filed these reports. The letters had no punctuation, they were full of grossly misspelled words, and words were not capitalized. A representative report and the first letter from the untutored overseer was dated August 19, 1849, two months after Polk's death.

> Marm we have some sickness at this time but not dangerous the crop
> is doing well at this time we have had a fine spell wether on the coten
> crop the corne crop is good if we have nomis for tune we will have ras a
> plenty of hogs for slaughter for the plantation we are now clearing more
> land making the servants winter clothing giting redy for the coten as
> soon as it opens the stocks all lucks as well as cold be expected the death
> of my employure was veery unexpected and distresing to the negrose
> seamed to be much troubled a bout there master but sense they have
> heard they belong to you they are something beter reconciled the negros
> have behaved very well this year I have nothing more of interest your
> most obedient mairs[2]

116

Another letter from Mairs is dated September 20, 1849:

> *Marm i received your leter of the 4th of september we have had some sickness chills and feavors but the casis has bin mild they are all on the mend won or tow in the house but clear of feavor the corne crop is good but sense i rought you last the coten will not be as good as i thorte as the bold worms had bin opperating against it but i still think it is a far crop in the naberhood I think we will make the winter clothing for the negros in time we are gethering the coten and gining it you have not given me enny dy rections about your coten the president dy rection was this mark of coten in his name way it sends me the numbers and wats take the coten to troy put it in the ceere thomas w. beal i got mr j. t. leigh to ship it to picket perkins and company new orleans you will please give me some dy rections about the coten or anything else you want don we have packed 22 bals of coten i will send you the wats and number no name has been put on it yet The calculation is for me to stay heare another yeare respectfully*[3]

The overseer, in his illiterate style, appears to be an honest, conscientious employee. From 1849 until 1858 Mrs. Polk received regular reports. The letters are brief and difficult to decipher, but they relate the story of what happened on her Mississippi plantation.

Early in 1850 Sarah decided to visit the plantation herself and informed Mr. Mairs of her visit. The overseer replied in a letter dated March 15, 1850:

> *Marm i have received your leter dayted February the 22 the negros is behaving varry will the negros was muched pleased to hear you was coming doune to sey them they are all well at this tim though wone of them has dyed sense I rought to you last by the name of carline davis won that mr samuel phillips sent hear las april frome memphis this negro was diseased she come her sick and has bin complayming of and on ever sens she has bin heare she dyed the 21st of february bilous pneumonia we are going on with the plantation bisnass as well as we can planting corn and preparing to plant coten making the sume clothing for the negros the stock all luck as well as can be exspected the artikles you ordered up from new orleans have not arrived as yet as soon as the doug i will let you nough very respectfully*[4]

The overseer began his report with the health of the slaves, followed by a report on what he considered the other livestock. A doctor was called for a slave in case of serious illness and a midwife was provided at the time of birth.[5] It was thought that Sarah, however, was more concerned about the revenue from her plantation than she was about the well-being of her slaves. A well-fed, well-housed slave would be far more likely to be profitable to his owner.

Sarah's cotton crops sometimes were lost on the way to market when a boat was sunk or caught on fire. She had to learn about exchange rates and bank discounts. But even with the bad years, Sarah made a profit from the plantation. The New Orleans cotton broker recognized the Yelobusha cotton as being a superior type and paid a good price for it.

Polk's will made provisions that, if he survived Sarah, all of his slaves should be freed, but her slaves were not freed until the Civil War. By and large, Sarah was a better than average slave owner.

There are some aspects of Sarah's slave ownership, however, that are difficult to understand. First, there was a higher infant death rate among the slaves than was usually found. This is substantiated by reports from her overseer. It was usually attributed to the mother's neglect, but there is no report that Sarah made any move to improve the situation. Perhaps with her Calvinist beliefs she felt that it was pre-ordained.[6]

Sarah's grief and loneliness after James's death were great. Their togetherness and interdependence during 25 years of marriage was so marked it was inevitable that Sarah would experience a great loss. During the early months after James's death, Sarah went to Murfreesboro to visit her mother. Elizabeth Childress was very perceptive and recognized Sarah's need. She urged Sarah to take her namesake, little Sally — Sarah Jetton — to live with her. Mrs. Childress took her great-grandchild to Polk Place and left her in Sarah's care. It had been the dying wish of Sarah's niece that Sarah take her daughter to live with her, and the former first lady was very happy to welcome this little child into her home. Judge John Catron had earlier advised Sarah that her previous interests and manner of living had not fitted her to raise a child. However, Sarah retained a fine nurse who took good care of Sally, who brightened the lives of everyone at Polk Place.[7]

In the spring of 1849 there were floods in Tennessee and the summer was very hot. Cholera struck Nashville in July and those who were able to do so fled the city. Sarah, who had lost her husband to this dread disease, had a great fear for both herself and Sally. So she and the child left Nashville and went to visit friends in Columbia and Murfreesboro until the epidemic waned.

Cholera had been known in the Mississippi Valley since 1832 and had occurred in waves until 1850 and thereafter. The infecting organism, vibrio cholerae, could be retained in the body for several months after the patient had recovered. Such carriers could then be instrumental — through infected food or water — in starting a new wave of the illness.

Sarah had never moved her church membership from Columbia, even while she was in Washington. She did attend the First Presbyterian Church in Nashville after the Polks made their first home there. The Reverend Edgar, pastor of the church in Nashville, was most anxious to have Sarah as a member. He asked her repeatedly to move her membership, but she always refused, using as an excuse that she did not want her name to be read out in church. Finally, Edgar was successful in changing her mind. On a visit to Polk Place, he told Sarah that her church in Columbia had burned, along with the records of membership. Sarah was persuaded by this argument. Soon after this event she transferred her membership from Columbia to Nashville, where she attended for her remaining years.[8]

After Polk's death, it became a custom for all members of the state legislative body to call as a group upon the widow of the former president on New Year's Day. The time was later changed by a resolution of both houses to any suitable day on which the House was meeting.[9] Other organizations in the city of Nashville and elsewhere considered it a duty and a privilege to visit Polk Place, where they would pay homage to the first lady and visit Polk's tomb. The participants of civic and military parades and processions uncovered their heads as they marched by her home. Sarah, and any guests who happened to be present, would go to the gate to watch the procession. At times the military procession would pause and salute Mrs. Polk and she would acknowledge this recognition.[10]

The extravagant praise heaped on Sarah must have been deserved, because it came from many sources and many distinguished persons. In fact, there is no record of any president's wife receiving so many honors after her husband's death. Few men of distinction who visited Nashville failed to call at Polk Place to pay homage to the former first lady. Sarah was said to be always willing to converse, but she was reluctant and sparing about discussing events in her own life. Most information available about the life of Sarah comes not from her own words but from those of her friends and associates, found in letters among her papers and elsewhere. She was never seen in public except when she attended church. She received many visitors to Polk Place but never returned the visits, although from time to time she did visit friends and relatives in Columbia and Murfreesboro.[11]

There were those who were critical of Sarah's election to go into seclusion after her husband's death, and who suggested that she might have used her talents and influence to attain greatness. She chose rather to be the representative of her husband's name and greatness and was satisfied to rest in his shadow.[12] This could imply that she had always remained in her husband's shadow, but evidence points to something else: that she, as his only confidante and advisor, had truly earned her own place in history.

Sarah, as the president's widow, received a tremendous amount of mail from friends, families, and the many associates of her husband. She felt an obligation to answer all letters, fueled by her great desire that her husband's memory should be preserved in every way possible. Although she at first had to bear the considerable expense of postage, Sarah became the first president's widow to receive franking privileges, which permitted her to send her mail anywhere in the United States without paying postage. She was required only to place her signature at the top of an envelope.[13]

Sarah's experience as confidante and secretary to Polk led her — perhaps more than any other first lady — to recognize the value of all papers and letters connected with the career of her husband. The mementos were preserved, and Sarah realized that the letters, papers, and manuscripts were material from which future historians could weave the history of her husband's career. Ultimately, the papers were placed in the Library of Congress.[14]

On November 2, 1850, two of Sarah's nieces, Johanna and Sarah Rucker, who had visited for prolonged periods in the White House while Sarah was the first lady, were married in a splendid double wedding. Johanna married little Sally's father, Robert Jetton, and Sarah married James Phillips. The brides were daughters of Sarah Polk's sister Susan, Mrs. William Reed Rucker.

After James's death Sarah rarely went any place except to church. In 1850 Jenny Lind, known as the Swedish Nightingale, came to Nashville to give a concert. Dr. Rucker and Susan Rucker were visiting at Polk Place at that time and they urged Sarah to attend the concert, but she would not.[15]

In June 1852 grief came to Sarah again when her niece Sarah Rucker Phillips died in childbirth. The baby survived the mother by only a few days. And as if Mrs. Polk had not experienced enough grief, Johanna Rucker Jetton died in October, also in childbirth. The baby, a little girl, survived. Sarah's favorite nieces, who had been married in a double wedding, were buried with the same burial rites.[16]

Sarah continued her efforts to preserve Polk history, especially the part her husband had played during his long political career. Appreciative of those who had collected relics, letters, and other items relevant to preserving the record of that era, Sarah not only amassed much material of value to future historians but she was also a generous contributor to the Tennessee Historical Society, donating many valuable artifacts. These included a medallion likeness of President Polk; a blue pitcher used in the Indian Council that met in 1785 at Hopewell and originally owned by Oken-Shan-Tah, the great chief of the Cherokees; and an Indian pipe and ornaments given to James Polk by Wee-No-Shick, chief of the Winnebagos. Other articles added to this remarkable collection were the four gospels in Cherokee; a piece of live oak from the ship *Constitution*, carved into the form of a book; one of Polk's hickory canes, which had been presented to him by the "Castile" Hickory Club of New York; and a medallion likeness of Louis-Philippe, dated 1846.[17]

By the early 1850s Major Daniel Graham and Major John Childress had become involved as Sarah's business advisers, but Sarah herself did not cease to be interested and active in her business affairs, since she still received monthly reports from Mr. Mairs. Sarah's slaves were allowed to raise some cotton on their own, and the accounts show that their share of the proceeds was fairly distributed. Other items for household use, such as blankets, were of good material. Their clothing was woven and sewn on the plantation. Sickness and mortality on the plantation were faithfully reported by Mairs in his letters to Mrs. Polk.[18]

Mairs sent another letter to Sarah dated November 6, 1850:

> *Marm i have just received a leter from major Daniel graham stating that he exspected to visit your farm sometime in december next he wishes to nough whether or not i have muls anof to surply the plantation i purchased a mul last may give $95 for him we have a plenty of muls at present but 30 of them are giting old and jaded and muls are selling high at present and i nough leave it with you to say whether or not it would be beter to part with the old wons and Buy more or not i*

will wait for an ancer from you youre servants crope of coten in 1849
was about 8400 lbs of sead coten youre people are all well at present evy
has lost both of hir youngest children we are nough gethering the crop of
coten we have picked 67 bags and have 90 or 95 bags out i think we
will make a 175 bals waing 400 pounds each we have gethered a part of
the corn i think we will make plenty for the youse of the plase we have
75 head of hogs to slaughter i think this will surply the plase plentfully

At this time, Mairs continued to be concerned about the status of
his position as overseer:

> *To Mrs. Sarah Polk*
> *Marm I dough not recol lect being employed by you or eny agent of*
> *yours for another yeare though the way mager graham rits he expects me*
> *to remain as i supposed i had writen to you before nough would*
> *exspected major graham heare by this time i am willing to remane in*
> *your business if it is satisfactory but i think the present prises of coten*
> *will justyfy me to cal on you to ras my salary allso i have receved 6*
> *addishalnal hands and a blacksmith sense my wages was raseed i would*
> *of made this request last year but things seam to be in confusion i will*
> *be satisfide with youre oppinion or major graham your most obedient*[19]

One black woman, Marrick, was taught to weave. Another slave,
Harry, the plantation blacksmith, learned to read and write while in
Tennessee. Harry wrote a letter to Mrs. Polk that indicated that the
slaves had some degree of affection for their owner. This letter is the
only one known to have been written to the Polks by a slave from the
plantation.

> *Dear Master, As a servant I want to subscribe my friendship to you*
> *and family as I am still in Carralton yet and doing good labor for my*
> *imploieer he feeds me well and don't work me tow hard. I would wish*
> *to be remembered to all of my people old mistrs [Jane Polk] esphirly.*
> *Tell the old lady Harry is her servant until deth. I would be glad to see*
> *hir one mor time. Dear master I look for you of February but you never*
> *come up to Carrlton.*
> *Dear master I have a 11 children. I have been feitheful over the anvill-*
> *block evr cen 1811 and is still old Harry My childrens names daniel,*
> *morcel [Marshall], ben, elis, carrell, charles, elushers, david, moonrey*
> *[Monroe], carline, opheller some requests from you please to send me a*
> *letter how all the people are doing in your country rect your letter to mr.*
> *edward t davidson carrollton mississippi harry your servant*[20]

A letter from Mairs to Sarah at a later date related that old Harry, in addition to smithing on the plantation, had plied his trade elsewhere and gained a profit of $487.76 for his owner.[21]

James Polk, it is true, had not at heart been a constitutionalist. He is quoted as having said, "I put my face alike against southern agitation and northern fanatics."[22]

As early as 1826, in a debate in the House over slavery, he made the observation that when the United States became free, "This species of population was found among us. It had been entailed upon us by our ancestors, and was viewed as a common evil affecting the whole nation. Some of the states which then possessed it have since gotten rid of it. They were a species of property that differed from all others. They were rational; they were human beings."

When Polk retired from the presidency in 1849, he was gloomy over the prospect of maintaining the institution of slavery in the future. He felt that the differences between North and South over slavery "would be attended with terrible consequences to the country and cannot fail to destroy the Democratic Party, if it does not ultimately destroy the union itself."[23]

Thus, Polk's main concern was the preservation of the Union and the Constitution. If the Union could not be preserved, any discussion over slavery was fruitless.

In 1852 Franklin Pierce was elected the fourteenth president of the United States. Pierce was a dark-horse candidate just as James had been. Polk had commissioned Pierce as a colonel in the Mexican War.[24]

The many letters to Sarah Polk concerning her plantation slaves reveal different views of that sad part of U.S. history. One such letter was written by John Bills to Mrs. Polk, dated January 28, 1852:

> *Dear Madam*
> *I am advised by our mutual friend James Walker, Esquire that by the lamented death of your good old mother-in-law Mrs. Jane Polk, my ward, Marshall T. Polk is entitled to two negroes, a man and a woman and perhaps children, which he says are at your plantation in Mississippi.*
> *My object in addressing you is to know your wishes on the subject of retaining them for the present year and if so to settle the amount of hire if (as in the case of Bob) you do not desire the use of them, you will send me an order for them that I may have them removed to this place.*
> *With best wishes for your health and happiness I am very truly your obedient servant.*

Here, to Sarah's credit, she replied to express her wish to exchange Charles, his wife Lucy, and their two children, so that they would be able to remain with their friends in Mississippi. Marshall Polk, a cadet at West Point, wrote that he wished done what was best for humanity's sake. For some unknown reason, Sarah's and Marshall's wishes were not carried out. The slaves were sent to Bolivar, Tennessee, in April. Bills wrote that the move had caused a lot of unhappiness by the separation of the slaves from their friends and relatives, and he added that he would try to make some changes that would relieve the distress of the slaves.[25]

This exchange would seem to indicate that some slave owners and plantation managers might have some regard for the feelings of slaves, but that such feelings could be overridden by the profit motive.

There was much sickness from time to time at Sarah's Mississippi plantation. Mairs wrote on August 3, 1852, as follows: "Marm we have some sickness won of the little boys by the name of william dyed the 18 of july some of the children have whoping colf this time the doct sayed william dyed with pneumonia." This letter was followed by another from Mairs two weeks later, a little earlier than was customary.

> *August 18, 1852*
> *Marm,*
> *I nough write you a few lins concerning youre plantation and people we had some sickness and have lost two of the children sens i rote you last daphny youngist child by the name of maryan and mariea davis his youngist child by the name of juoyan dyed with whoping cough seems to have a sor thot with it the whoping cough has bin vary destrucktive among the children in this naborhood we have it nough but it sams to be some milder not much feavor the crop of corn is very good the best i have had sense i have bin on the plase the coten crop is good oup to this date and if we have a good fall and it matures well if we all have good helth it will put us oup to save it if bids far for a large crop we have made some clothing and have clearned some land we are nough preparing for gethging coten the stocks all lucks as well as could be expected most obedient*[26]

The letters from Mairs always reported the physical condition of the slaves on the Mississippi plantation and the occasional outbreaks of communicable disease that ran unchecked and were more lethal than would ordinarily be expected. A letter that followed the one of August

1852 by six weeks was undoubtedly written by someone more literate than Mairs, and although the letter is signed by Mairs, it was evidently written by the doctor in attendance:

> *We have had for the past week or two a great deal of sickness. The children have whooping cough — all doing well except one Eva's child, which will probably die in consequence of deep seated disease of the lung. Among the grown ones Giles William Nevils, Carolyn Harris and old Cloe have been very sick but are now improving. Henry was severely attacked with pneumonia on last Friday — his disease seemed to be giving way under treatment until yesterday evening when he suddenly got worse and died today. They all have an affection of the throat which is unattended with pain, but is of a firey redness which in some cases spreads suddenly and rapidly through the system extending to the stomach and through the bowels and also into the lungs, etc. etc. with excessive perspiration, great prostration, collapse and a speedy death. This was the case with Henry. The others will have the sore throat, though they do not seem to be aware of it, but with them it does not get worse or spread. It is in the large number of cases relieved by swabbing the throat with spts turpentine or solution lunar caustic and external rubefacient applications. The doctor calls it erysipelas or Saint Anthony's fire of the internal organs. It has been prevalent in the country for the last year or two, and he thinks most of the deaths that have occurred from pneumonia in this section within that time have been in consequence of this sudden extension of erysipelas to all the organs of the system. We are making a tolerably fine crop of cotton and have been gathering very well until the recent interruption from sickness. Have seventy bales packed. Most obedient*[27]

The disease described by the writer was undoubtedly due to hemolytic streptococcus. The type of onset, the appearance of the throat, and the extension to other areas of the body fit what is called strep throat. At that time there was no effective treatment and, in an epidemic, severe and even lethal infections would occur.

Chapter 10

It was natural that Sarah — as former first lady, and widely acclaimed as such — would be approached by friends and acquaintances who wished her to use her influence in getting favors from those in authority. Randall McGavock, son of Louis McGavock and grandson to the Polks' dear friend Felix Grundy, came to Polk Place in February 1853 seeking a letter of recommendation to President Franklin Pierce. Sarah complied and addressed a note to the president:

> Mrs. Polk takes pleasure in presenting to the consideration of President Pierce her friend Mr. R. W. McGavock of Nashville, Tennessee. Mr. McGavock is a highly educated gentleman, has spent much time traveling in Europe, and is the grandson of the late Honorable Felix Grundy.
>
> Will the President be pleased to accept Mrs. Polk's assurance of respect.
>
> Polk Place, Nashville, Tennessee
> February 19, 1853[1]

Dr. J. G. M. Ramsey in his *Autobiography and Letters* (1866) related that his son John Closure Ramsey was also a beneficiary of Sarah's intercession. John Ramsey, a close friend of the Polks, worked on James's behalf during the 1844 presidential campaign. Dr. Ramsey described in a letter the story of his son's capture and imprisonment by the North during the Civil War. At the surrender of Vicksburg, General Ramsey had been paroled but not exchanged, and he was recaptured while undergoing treatment for severe disabilities. Imprisoned at Knoxville, Tennessee, he suffered greatly. An invalid who was unable to work, he was marched in ball and chains along with the other prisoners. Finally hospitalized and released, Ramsey opened a law practice in Knoxville. But a writ was issued for his arrest and he would have been sent to a Northern prison had not Sarah Polk intervened.[2]

Nashville suffered a disaster in the spring of 1855 when a tornado hit the city. Numerous large mansions were destroyed and many of its citizens were injured. The copper roof of the state capitol building was ripped away by the force of the storm, and a similar fate befell the tin roof of the First Presbyterian Church. At Polk Place the high winds leveled several trees, but no one was injured. A friend of the Polks, Vernon Stevenson, came by to check on the people at Polk Place. With him he brought additional bad news. When the tornado struck the state penitentiary, fires broke out in the shops and all of the shops and the roof of one wing were destroyed.[3]

Despite the turmoil that such an event created, the city gradually returned to normal, including the annual visitation of neighbors on New Year's Day. Mrs. Polk had two very distinguished callers that year: General Sam Houston, an old friend of the Polks, and Randall McGavock, who had recently had a popular book published on his European travels.[4]

It is regrettable that Sarah was not as willing to put pen to paper as was her husband, a man who wrote many volumes of letters and diaries that contain more verbiage than substance by far. Her letters — at least while her husband was living and politically active — do, however, reveal much about Sarah herself. After her husband died and she became a semi-recluse, we find little in her correspondence that follows any continuous thread of her life at Polk Place. Sarah's papers, which in themselves are almost indecipherable, are of little help. The papers concern themselves to a great extent with what was happening on her cotton plantation in Mississippi. In fact, the letters from John Mairs to Sarah reveal a great deal more about the life on the plantation and about her involvement in the management of the farm than did Sarah's letters. So we are left to deduce most of what we know about her from the letters of others. One is led to believe that Sarah was much more concerned about preserving an image of James than she was in creating one of and for herself.

In August 1853 Randall McGavock married Seraphine Derry of Allisonia. The Rev. Edgar performed the marriage ceremony and paid a call on Sarah a few days afterward to tell her about the wedding. The conversation took place in the beautiful garden at Polk Place. As they walked and talked, little Sally was playing nearby.

Around this time, Sarah learned there were rumors afloat that connected her romantically with James Buchanan. She was quite indignant that anyone would for a moment believe she would have any such feelings about any man other than her late husband. She stated that she had too much respect for her beloved husband ever to change her name.[5]

Buchanan's acquaintance with Sarah Polk was a long-standing one. Simon Cameron, later a senator, had urged Buchanan in 1848 to campaign vigorously for James Polk in his home state of Pennsylvania so that in 1848 Polk would owe that state's support to him. Supreme Court Justice John Catron wanted Buchanan also to campaign in the west for Polk. The appeal to Buchanan to stump for Polk was his close friendship and admiration for Mrs. Catron and Mrs. Polk. These ladies repaid his good opinion with flattery and kindness.[6]

By 1856 Buchanan had made his decision to accept the nomination for president if offered by the Democrats at the June convention. On his return from England, where he had served as ambassador to the Court of St. James, he was amused by a newspaper clipping sent to him by Mrs. Sophia Plitt. The newspaper had reported that Buchanan would return by way of New Orleans in order to go to Tennessee to marry Mrs. Sarah Polk. Mrs. Plitt wrote jokingly she wished it were so. She was sure he would find it "an agreeable way of Polking your way into the presidency."[7]

Buchanan, like Polk, developed a strong distaste for the presidency and politics in general. One of his supporters had, through an article to the *Pittsburgh Post*, planted the idea that he wanted to run for a second term. Subsequently, the president wrote a statement that he positively would not accept the renomination. He told Sarah Polk, "I am now in my sixty-ninth year and am heartily tired of my position as President."[8]

Instead of romance, much of Sarah's thought was given to her cotton plantation in Mississippi. She was a shrewd businesswoman and her plantation was a paying enterprise.[9] The profits varied from year to year, depending on pests and weather conditions. One letter from Mairs in August 1855 tells of the uncertainties that could plague growers.

> *Mairm inough write you a few lins your "servants" are all well at present your woman eve increased HIR family on 16th calds hir child henry polk we have had some dry wether sens irote you the coten opnnen vary fast the hands has picked finely the crop of coten has BIN cut short by the bold worm ihear goodeal of complaint in this naberhood and idough not think will make a large crop nough but istill hope we will*

*make a FAR crop the corn is made it is good we had a fine rane last
EVENIG which will help the coten and pee crop and the potaters the
stocks all lucks as well as cold be expested i will dough my best respect-
fully*[10]

Dr. Richard Bardolph, a distinguished scholar who has written
definitive works on slavery, relates that the genteel slave overseers rather
studiously avoided the term "slave" in their writing and polite conversations. We supposed that Sarah, in writing to Mairs, did not use the
word "slave," and in responding, he also avoided the term.[11]

On November 7, 1855, Mairs again wrote to Mrs. Polk:

> *Mairm inough write you a few lins your servants are all well at pres-
> ent we hald 10 bags of your coten to troy today and will hall about 80
> bags before we stop we will stop then unteel we ship some we have had a
> good deal of raine and the rivir is in good order for boting the steamer
> Unicorn has bin up all the summer we will go out this rise is asking 4
> dollars per bag ithink that is rather high coten is low perhaps we will
> dough beter yet on this rise your coten is in the care of powell and
> trummel troy mississippi we have a great deal of coten to pick out yet
> the negros behave themselves vary well we are doing the best we can
> write me when you git this leter vary respectfully*[12]

In 1857, Sarah was 54 years of age and still continued her usual
way of life at Polk Place. That winter was a very cold one, so cold that
the Cumberland River froze over and a canal had to be cut through
the ice so that the boats could pass.

Sally, Sarah's ward, was now 17 and attracted young friends who
came to make Polk Place more lively. The mayor of Nashville was
Sarah's friend, Randall W. McGavock. The *Nashville Daily News* carried the following item on December 1858: "Thirty-four years ago,
1824, Randall McGavock was mayor of Nashville, a village containing
about 4,500 persons, without even a turnpike approaching it. Now his
grandnephew, Randall W. McGavock, is mayor of Nashville, a city of
thirty thousand inhabitants, approached at three points by railroad and
with several others in contemplation. What Nashville may be thirty-
four years hence none of us can realize in our highest anticipation of
progress."[13]

Laura Carter Holloway, a visitor at the residence of Governor A. V.
Brown, wrote a letter about Polk Place and Sarah.

Meeting Mrs. Polk is like seeing the original of a familiar picture, and in a few moments after seeing her, we are surprised to find ourselves forgetting any confident feeling we are conversing with the lady who has presided at the executive mansion with a wider popularity than has since been obtained by any one of her successors. She seems to have a warm and unwavering sympathy in the success of others, and in her conversation there is an expression of those affectionate sympathies which made her beloved in a more elevated sphere. She has a pleasing figure, what we call lady-like, delicate, erect, and graceful, with a great deal of manner, in the last respect resembling the late Mrs. Madison. Mrs. Polk's mental endowments, as well as her personal qualities, combine to render her a general favorite, while her manners and character give a permanence to her social success by converting admirers into friends.[14]

Laura Holloway, who visited many times with Sarah, had first-hand knowledge of her that few other writers were privileged to experience. We have wondered why, after James Polk died, we have seen so little correspondence from her. Holloway helps to clarify this matter. "Mrs. Polk, ever willing to converse, and always enriching the conversation, is remarkably reticent in regard to her own life. Her most familiar friends fail to persuade an account of incidents relating purely to herself; and it is only by the casual letters of visitors and the few descriptions of some friends that anything is known."[15]

In the summer of 1859 the Chatham Artillery, then commanded by Captain Claghorn, was greeted by crowds of citizens and the cadets from the local military institute. They were honored with a welcoming address by the mayor and a 31-gun salute at the capitol. Returning to their hotel, they passed by the home of Sarah Polk. The writer of this anecdote, a member of the artillery, noted that a feeling of sadness seemed to overcome the corps and that as they came to present arms, they knew that they were paying a small token of respect to the late president."[16]

Sarah's enterprise in Mississippi was attended with various shades of fortune. Her overseer was not lacking in effort; however, in some of his last letters there is a note of discouragement that was perhaps justified. Each year he had proposed to have a good crop, but frequently he had met failure. The crop of 1857 was somewhat below the average. Excessive rain and then drought seemed to conspire against success. The boll weevil also intervened to greatly reduce the crop. There was always the possibility that the poor health of the slaves might make the planting and harvesting much more difficult. It was indeed the misfortune of both overseer and owner that the one abundant cotton crop during his stewardship was marred by the bad health of the slaves and the bad weather at harvest time, so that at least 30 bales rotted in the field.[17]

We may never know exactly why Mrs. Polk sold most of her Mississippi plantation in 1860. It is possible that the recurring problems of raising cotton encouraged her to relinquish this enterprise. Indeed, it is possible that the risk and disappointment that were expressed in Mairs's letters were enough to bring Sarah to such a decision.

Sarah was very knowledgeable about the events in the world outside of Polk Place. She was aware of the threatening rhetoric of secessionists and the equally bombastic ranting of the abolitionists. This fiery controversy carried within it the threat of strife. The Nashville mayor, Randall McGavock, came quite often to visit her at Polk Place. He came as a friend, but he also liked to sound out Sarah on national and political news. It was during one such visit that Sarah asked McGavock if he expected to run again for mayor. He responded that he would not run again, stating that he sensed the country was so divided that it could expect difficult times. They then discussed John Brown's raid on Harpers Ferry and its political significance. Both Sarah and McGavock were fearful of the outcome. On that same visit McGavock told Sarah that he had heard she had sold her plantation. Sarah replied that she had indeed sold most of it, and she added that there was so much unrest in both North and South she feared that some day she might not be able to continue as an absentee owner. McGavock told Sarah that he felt she had done a wise thing.

The fears of Sarah and McGavock came to realization on April 12, 1861, when Fort Sumter came under fire from secessionist troops in Charleston, South Carolina. Surrender of the fort by Major Robert Anderson came after the garrison had been under fire for 30 hours. President Abraham Lincoln issued his proclamation calling for 75,000 militia to suppress the rebellion. So then rhetoric was replaced with guns. The war came to Nashville immediately and the enlistment of troops began on April 20, 1861. Five days later Tennessee declared that it was seceding from the Union. Polk had been a Union man and a strict constitutionalist, but he was also an ingrained Southerner and a slave holder. Either choice — to declare for the Union or for the

South — would have caused him great distress. Sarah must have felt some relief that her cherished husband was spared from making such a choice.

Sarah made no outright choice and declared herself to be neutral. When the war erupted, Nashville had a population of 17,000. It was the largest city south of the Ohio River except for New Orleans. Much freight was transported by railroads and by water on the Cumberland River. Fort Donaldson on the Cumberland and Fort Henry on the Tennessee were outposts intended to protect Nashville, which had become a vital supply depot and transfer point.[18] Nashville was of great strategic importance to the South. However, when Fort Donaldson fell, the city became untenable by the confederates.

News of Fort Donaldson's fall came to Nashville on February 16, 1863, and immediately the population was thrown into a panic. Many inhabitants made great haste to abandon the city with whatever possessions could be carried by carriage or wagon.[19] But others, who had no definite destination in mind, wandered in an aimless and confused fashion up and down the streets. Mobs looted government warehouses and steamboats, carrying off huge supplies of bacon, salt pork, flour, blankets, and clothing. These wandering crowds forcibly took over horses and wagons to haul away the plunder.[20] A newspaper reporter was amazed to see that the mobs included "Negroes, Irish laborers, and even genteel looking persons."[21]

It was two days later that General Nathan Bedford Forrest arrived with his cavalry and put an end to the looting. Forrest's cavalry used army wagon trains to retrieve the remaining stores, the wagon trains then moving to Murfreesboro to join General Johnston. It was in this state that Nashville awaited the arrival of the Union troops.

General Buell was the commander of the Union occupying force. Soon after his arrival, Buell sent Mrs. Polk a formal note requesting permission to call on her at Polk Place. She immediately responded in writing that she would see him and his staff on the following morning. Promptly at the designated time, General Buell arrived with several of his staff and nearly all of the commanding generals in the area. Sarah had enlisted some of her friends and neighbors to aid her in receiving and entertaining the visiting military. The hour was spent pleasantly, and on leaving the officers expressed their pleasure at the kind reception.[22]

Later on, Sarah received General William Sherman as a visitor. When she entered the parlor to speak to the general, he first turned to her and said that he had been looking at Polk's inaugural address, which hung over the mantel. He told the former first lady that the address contained an expression of attachment and loyalty to the Union, but it also affirmed that such loyalty should be preserved forever indissoluble. Sarah, ever tactful and always able to give an apt reply, told the general that those were good sentiments for even today. General Sherman, probing further, asked her if she were to go to Washington, where would she go first? She replied that she would go first to the White House to call on the president. The answer came as a surprise to the general, who was aware of the distaste most Southerners had for Lincoln. Sarah said that she was indeed loyal to her homeland and people, but that the principles of honor and truth that she held would preserve her from bigotry and partisanship.[23]

The former first lady had made a calm, wise decision. She was never once threatened, and the Union officers were deferential in their treatment of her. Her prolonged training in tact and diplomacy served her well. She was never demanding in her requests and did not try to presume on her former position as first lady. On one occasion, Sarah's mother became ill and Sarah requested transportation to Murfreesboro to visit and help care for her. The Union command honored her request by providing an ambulance with a guard and an officer for escort. After Sarah returned to Nashville, officers stationed near Murfreesboro continued to provide her with information on the state of her mother's health.[24] No one contested Sarah's stand that she was neutral. Both Union and Confederate officers were at times visitors to Polk Place and were graciously received. Neither she nor her property were ever harmed in any way. She saw many of her friends and relatives leave to join the Confederate army. Her nephew, John Whitsett, Jr., paid her a farewell visit: he was only 16 and a student at the Western Military Institute. Sarah tried hard to persuade him to remain in school, but he pleaded loyalty to the South and the need for every man to enter the war and thus end it sooner. Johnny was wounded four times during the war but survived. Another nephew, Eliash Whitsett, also volunteered and joined the Second Tennessee Regiment. He was to die of a wound sustained at Shiloh.[25]

The story of what happened in Nashville and of the privations endured by its inhabitants during the Civil War shows that the hardships were not borne equally. Sarah's status as former first lady of a constitutionalist husband and a dyed-in-the-wool Southern slave holder must have given the Union command in Nashville some pause about this remarkable lady, who being neither fish nor fowl must have generated some concern about how she should be handled.

An Englishman, Henry Yates Thompson, while visiting in Nashville wrote in his diary on November 17, 1863, about a visit to Mrs. Polk:

> *Dr. J. B. Lindsay [Chancellor of the University of Tennessee] took me into the house to call on Mrs. Polk — A well preserved woman whose conversation was most interesting. She had lived a long time in Washington and knew Calhoun intimately. At the time of Lincoln's election she was in Mississippi and said to a gentleman who had been pressing to see her that she was a submissionist, as those in the South were called who were for opposition through the ballot and legal means alone. The gentleman drew back amazed and disgusted. She said she greatly blames the men in the Democratic Party for the war because they divided their forces in the 1860 election instead of following one man as they should have done. The gentleman went further to note that she often goes to Murfreesboro and says that since that battle it has been a scene of desolation, not a fence, scarcely a tree standing. She told me as a piece of secret history known to few that Mr. Calhoun had wanted to continue in office under her husband. When he, Calhoun, came to bid her a farewell she had said she hoped he would go to England as minister, but he was for staying and working for the South. She said he was a charming man and a great talker. She and her husband had messed with him for three years in Washington — at that time the politicians were to club together for their meals.*[26]

Thompson wrote his diary at the age of 24, during a visit to North America. His diaries covered five months of war: July 10 to December 13, 1863. It is apparent that Sarah would have liked the election of 1860 to have turned out differently. She wished that life, as the Southern elite knew it, could continue.

A description of Nashville during the Civil War by a nurse, Elvira Powers, gives more insight than some other works written about that city. Powers was commissioned on April 1, 1864, and ordered to report for duty for hospital service at the front in Nashville. She determined that she would keep a diary so that posterity would know about her experience. She made revealing observations on the care received by the sick and wounded military, and about civilian life in the occupied city during that conflict. "Nashville is a city which is set upon hills. It is also founded on a rock, and the fact that it has not much earth upon that rock has made the pretext for leaving numberless deceased horses and mules upon the surface without even a heathen burial." She noted that "Nashville was also a city of narrow filthy streets and in some localities the water, which like the offense of the King of Denmark, smells to heaven." She stated that the agent of the Christian Commission, the Reverend E. P. Smith, had said, "It is astonishing how much one dead mule one may breathe and yet survive. It is a city of either dust or mud."[27]

Since Sarah left her home only on Sunday to attend church, she saw and experienced few of the difficulties that beset most of the citizens of Nashville. Leading a protected existence, she would occasionally be called on by some of her friends for aid. Colonel Joseph Alexander Ackland and his wife, Adelicia, lived on a magnificent estate called the Belmont Mansion: said to be the finest of antebellum homes. Following the Union occupation of Nashville, Mrs. Ackland came to visit Sarah and told her that she needed help. Her husband had left Belmont and gone to Louisiana to look after plantation business and now Belmont was partially occupied by Union officers. Rumors had come to Mrs. Ackland that there would soon be a battle near Belmont and Nashville and there was some fear of looting. She asked Sarah if she might presume on their friendship to bring her valuables to Polk Place. Sarah readily agreed and stated that she had already become custodian of some objects of the Tennessee Historical Society. A soldier came with a large number of portraits, fine paintings, silver, and jewelry.[28]

In some instances Sarah had difficulty in dealing with the occupying military forces. She was informed at one time that she would be able to purchase coal, as other Nashville civilians could, by taking the oath of allegiance to the Union. Mrs. Polk tried to get coal from other sources, remarking that her husband had been president of the whole United States, so she could not support any one party over the other.[29]

On October 10, 1864, Elvira Powers called on Mrs. Polk to obtain some leaves and flowers to keep as souvenirs of Polk Place. The flowers were to be placed on paper as an exhibit for the sanitary fair. She recorded in her diary that Mrs. Polk received her kindly and cordially. Sarah went with Elvira to the grounds and cut the leaves and flowers for the visitor herself. She also presented Elvira with a photograph of Polk Place taken from Vine Street, which showed the tomb of the former president.[30]

Elvira noted that Mrs. Polk had not entered society since the death of President Polk, and she continued her writing with a description of the former first lady. Sarah, at the time of Powers's observation, was 61 and was to live nearly 27 more years. "In person she is a trifle above the medium height, slender, with a high forehead, delicate features, and bears marks of taste and refinement."[31]

While Sarah was leading a relatively serene existence inside the haven of Polk Place, there was a war going on almost within cannon shot of her home. By late November 1864 General John Hood had brought his army (after defeat in Atlanta) by a very circuitous route to the outskirts of Nashville. The first battle of any magnitude was fought on November 30 at Franklin, just 10 miles south of Nashville. The Union forces under General John Schofield after five hours of fierce fighting retreated to the fortifications of Nashville. The price paid by the Confederates fighting under Hood was great. Union troops fighting behind breastworks had a loss of just over 2,000 men, but the assaulting force of Confederates lost almost 3 times that number in dead and wounded. This was, after the awful attrition suffered by the rebel armies, a staggering loss. In similar battles fought in the Civil War, none exceeded the losses in dead and wounded sustained in the Battle of Franklin. Besides the six Confederate generals who died, one was captured and three others were so badly wounded that they never returned to the army.[32]

At that time Sarah Polk was an observer in the eye of the storm. She undoubtedly heard the roar of the cannonade and saw the flash from the fire of the big guns.

On the field at Franklin the carnage defied description. Soldiers in Hood's assaulting army characterized the scene as indescribable. A private wrote later, "I cannot describe it. It beggars description, I will not describe it." A colonel on Stewart's staff wrote to his wife, "I am tired of the sickening details. You can see our dreadful loss from published accounts." These were men who had seen four years of war.[33] The six dead Confederate generals were treated deferentially and were moved to Carnton Place, the mansion owned by Colonel Randall McGavock, and placed side by side on the wide back gallery.[34]

In the aftermath of the debacle at Franklin in December 1864, Hood chose to march his decimated army on Nashville. The die-hard Southerners in that city were jubilant at the prospect of seeing the Yankees chased out, but their celebration was short-lived. The defeat of the Confederate army was total. In that engagement Thomas employed over 70,000 men; his loss in killed and wounded were less than 4,000. General Hood, with just over 23,000 men, listed his casualties at around 1,500. This was the last major battle in the Civil War that was fought on Tennessee soil. The army of Tennessee was finished as an effective fighting force and Hood's figures on the losses in that battle were a gross understatement.[35]

The war left the city of Nashville in ruins. The gutters of most streets were stopped, creating marked overflows in wet seasons. Over half of the trees in Nashville were destroyed, while more than 200 homes were destroyed and replaced by fortifications. Buzzards in great numbers were attracted to the odor of dead mules. There was a small-pox outbreak of epidemic proportions, and there were many other diseases prevalent and no medicine to treat the sick.[36] The *Nashville Daily Press* of May 3, 1864, reported, "More ardent spirits are consumed in Nashville than in Boston. The city is filled with thugs, robbers, highwaymen, and assassins. Murder stalks throughout the city almost every night."[37]

Although Sarah's property was unscathed by the war, the fate of her friends and relatives touched her intimately, particularly the death of her nephew Eliash and the wounding of John Whitsett, another nephew. In addition, she lost her dear friend Colonel Randall McGavock, who fought in the Tenth Tennessee Infantry Regiment, a unit that he himself had organized. He obtained the rank of colonel and was killed at Raymond, Kentucky, on May 12, 1863.

Chapter 11

The war ended for Nashville but the dreary years of reconstruction were still to be endured. Citizens of the city, weak and defeated, were prey to their victors, but not all of the predators were from the North. Indeed, many carpetbaggers were from the South. Brownlow, Tennessee's reconstructionist governor, set the tone for what was to come with his declaration: "As for the original conspirators who without provocation treacherously set the rebellion on foot, bad men who pressed it forward with all the malignancy of fiends and the cruelty of savages; who through rapine, arson, butchery and perjury fill the land with mourning, they are entitled to neither mercy nor forbearance."[1]

With the ending of the Civil War, Sarah entered the twilight years of her life. She was 62 two years of age and apparently in good health. Although she had led a protected existence throughout the war, she had sustained great losses of her financial assets. Her slaves were now free and cotton grown on the unsold portion of her cotton plantation was destroyed.

Almost one month before the war was officially ended at Appomattox, William (Parson) Brown was elected governor of Tennessee, and all the slaves in Tennessee were freed by a state constitutional amendment. At the next meeting of the state legislature the prewar custom of calling on the former president's lady was renewed. Colonel Bailie Peyton wrote Sarah a note informing her of their intended visit. His message was as follows:

> The General Assembly is mainly composed of those who well remember your association with distinguished personages of a past generation. How nobly you bore your part as attested by the unanimous voice of all. We would not recall the events of the last few years, but it is impossible that we could be insensible to these incidents which history will preserve when as we trust the calamities of that period are remembered no more. You were in the line of the advancing and receded hosts, in the very gulf stream of the war, but the mad passions

engendered by that conflict were ever calmed in the presence of your abode. Without reference to the flag he followed, each subordinate and superior regarded your feelings as sacred, and his good sword as pledged no less to your defense than to the cause in which he drew it. Candor, madam, compels us to say that we cannot dissever our veneration and regard for yourself from the grateful recollections we cherish for the memory of your distinguished husband. That spot which holds his remains, that tomb which is watched by such devoted affection, must be sacred in our eyes; it will be doubly so to posterity at a time far off as we trust, in the distant future, when your ashes shall mingle with his.[2]

This soaring prose describes precisely the regard and esteem with which Mrs. Polk was held. There is no evidence that any other U.S. citizen of prominence was able to sit astride the political fence and escape unscathed.

Even with the war over, Nashville was still to suffer some disasters. The recovery — as it was everywhere else in the South — was slow, and to compound the problem, only three months after the war the city of Nashville was to experience a devastating fire with the loss of vast amounts of government stores. A few months later another fire destroyed many houses in the residential area.[3]

In the summer of 1866 Nashville was revisited by an epidemic of cholera. The city had experienced serious epidemics of cholera before, but never so serious as the one of 1866. This severe outbreak was no doubt abetted by the deplorable sanitation prevailing in the city. That summer alone, out of a population of about 20,000, over 1,800 died in Nashville during a period of 6 weeks.[4]

Laura Carter Holloway felt that Sarah Polk's reputation and influence were so universal that she could have wielded a "mighty and beneficial influence" in post–Civil War days. The writer was disappointed that her contemporary chose to retire from such responsibility.

Holloway stated, "Had she chosen any art or mode of mediating the conditions of those around her, or of adorning and rendering attractive the social life in her home circle in the numberless ways which to one in her situation were easy and practical, the good she could have done would have been incalculable, but her morbid exclusiveness rendered her unsociable and her Christian virtues, too much inclined to austerity, closed her house to every form of gaiety."[5]

Instead of becoming a public figure, Sarah chose to become a recluse: the keeper of the shrine devoted to preserving the memory of her husband whose remains she had entombed on Polk Place.

Sarah did have others at Polk Place to take away some of the gloom that may have surrounded her. Little Sally, Sarah's niece, Sarah Polk Jetten, had grown up at Polk Place to become an attractive young woman who married George William Fall. But Sally had not wished to leave her home and Sarah wished her to stay. Mr. Fall was a prosperous businessman who had a good family background. Sally Fall gave birth to a baby girl named Saide Polk Fall and Polk Place was enriched by this new family.[6]

Sarah received many invitations from persons in high places to leave Polk Place and go visiting. President Andrew Johnson was among the presidents who extended invitations to her to visit the White House for a while and view the changes that had taken place since the Polks had left. Sarah declined all such invitations. She was kept well informed about life outside Polk Place by the numerous visitors who came there.

The American Association for the Advancement of Science met in Nashville in August 1877. The president of the association, Professor Simon Newcomb, made the following, somewhat derogatory, announcement: "The city of Nashville rejoices in something which heretofore we have been accustomed to associate only with the ancient world. This shrine all visitors are expected to worship. In accordance with this custom, which I am sure everyone present will recognize as becoming inappropriate, the Association will today, at the close of sectional business, proceed to pay their respect to Mrs. Polk, relict of the late President Polk."[7]

Professor Newcomb was referring to Mrs. Polk as if she were an organism that had survived in surroundings that had undergone great change. We visualize Sarah as one who was a faded custodian of what she had preserved as a large and stately tomb for James Polk. Sarah was indeed a part of the shrine. In November 1877 Holloway, who apparently knew the former first lady well, described her in her twilight years thus:

> She was born in the dawn of the nineteenth century, and is a pure type of a class which is rapidly becoming extinct. With her will pass away much of the excellence and not a few of the foibles of a class modeled after the aristocracy of this old world and their graftings in the new world.

Her life has been spent in an age and country where chivalric honor
to a woman is a matter of national pride, yet too 'tis a land of slaves
and slavery. The young and middle-aged of our day will never know
the opportunities of time and means which she, half a century ago,
enjoyed. For the south is changed, and verily all things have passed
away and all are new. The present generation, grown more on their
own resources and passing through the perplexities of change and misfortune will grow away from the old regime and perhaps lose many of
its virtues with too few of their faults.[8]

Holloway, while interpreting a woman and an age, was also cast-
ing herself in the role of a prophet.

The list of all the famous generals, judges, writers, and presidents
who came to call on Mrs. Polk in her late years was long and imposing. In late 1877 President and Mrs. Rutherford Hayes visited Sarah
at Polk Place during a Southern tour. With President and Mrs. Hayes
were Secretary of State William Everetts, Colonel Wade Hampton, and
Postmaster General Key. Mrs. Polk thought Mrs. Hayes a charming
woman. The presidential party was given a reception at the home of
Colonel E. W. Cole. But Sarah as usual declined the invitation to
attend.[9]

During Polk's presidency, Hayes's Whig Party — Hayes would later
recall with regret — had fallen into a period of discontent following the
election of Harrison in 1840, his death within one month, and the suc-
cession of John Tyler. Hayes admitted that his party had no positive
policy, or at least not an inspiring one. The Whigs' chief occupation
was criticizing President Polk, and they even fell to the level of chastis-
ing Mrs. Polk for being "too devout a Presbyterian," and for banning
the use of strong drink at White House parties.[10]

Mrs. Hayes, perhaps because of her husband's disputed election
in 1877, received harsher criticism than did Sarah Polk for her rules
banning the serving of alcoholic beverages in the White House.[11] She
came as near to any other first lady to the moral standards that Sarah
had set for conduct in the president's house in Washington. After breakfast Lucy Hayes had the family and the guests who happened to be present gather in the library to hear a chapter read from the Bible and to
say the Lord's Prayer.[12]

Temperance organizations did not have an opportunity to honor
Mrs. Hayes before she left the nation's capital. A group of temperance
women from Illinois, led by Anne Tressler Scott, presented Lucy with

six morocco-bound, gilt-edged, autographed albums and a pair of embroidered hangings for the Hayes' retirement home at Spiegel Grove. Over 2,600 signers returned the vellum sheets with their signatures and in some cases added sentimental lines or artistic illustrations. The first signature in the first volume was that of Sarah Polk.[13]

In September 1877 modern communication came to Polk Place: a telephone, the first ever to be installed in Nashville. The telephone had been installed three weeks before Rutherford Hayes visited Nashville. This simple device was made up of a magnet, a thin metallic plate, and a delicate wire, all housed in a box-like container. The experimental line was strung between Polk Place and the Adams home on the adjoining corner of Seventh Avenue North and Union Street. Mrs. Polk received the first message on September 1, 1877.[14] Several ladies and gentlemen of the Nashville community were invited to witness the introduction of this marvel. Sarah had a conversation with Professor Lovewell one block away at the Adams house.[15]

Sarah still welcomed all visitors to Polk Place and gave them a conducted tour through her shrine. Polk's study was exactly as he had left it many years before. She allowed no one to clean or dust inside it. Throughout the years she wore something of black in memory of her husband.[16]

Throughout the mansion the walls were covered with pictures, including numerous portraits of Sarah and James done by famous artists such as Earle and Healy. There were engravings and daguerreotypes of their relatives and friends. In the south parlor were portraits of Washington, Jefferson, Madison, John Quincy Adams, Jackson, and Polk.

Every room except the library was lined with mementos collected over the years. A tour of Polk Place resembled a tour through a museum. Cabinets displayed china, glass, reticules, watch fobs, and Indian handcrafts. Souvenirs covered the mantels. There was a nugget from the California gold field; an alabaster mold of Tom Thumb's foot; and the louis d'or presented to Sarah when she left Murfreesboro to go to the Moravian Female Academy in Salem, North Carolina, and the gavel used by Polk when he was Speaker of the House. Yet this mansion, housing a splendid display of Polk mementos, was not the main attraction of Polk Place. The visitor was dazzled by the beauty of the grounds: a sloping garden with large beds of verbenas, geraniums, heliotrope, and jessamine. In the center of this floral garden was the tomb of the ex-president.[17]

In the spring of 1880 Nashville celebrated its centennial: there was a parade with music and marching men who wore uniforms of past wars. A long procession made its way through the city and, following the Nashville tradition, Polk Place was in the line of march. Sarah and a group of children from grammar school stood at the Vine Street entrance of Polk Place and watched the parade go by. Led by their singing master, the children sang a centennial hymn.[18]

Sarah, the frequent recipient of letters that sang her praises, was honored in a letter from the Reverend Peschau, a former pastor of the German Lutheran Church in Nashville:

> *Dear and highly esteemed Mrs. Polk,*
> *Greetings in the name of our dear Lord, Jesus Christ. Last week I spent a few weeks in Charleston to attend the Annual Convention of the Lutheran Synod of South Carolina. It was my good fortune to be assigned to the house of William Kirkwood, Esquire, a venerable man 84 years of age. How well he remembers Mr. Polk's visit to the city on his return from Washington. It so happened that Mr. Polk was compelled to wait almost an hour directly in front of Mr. Kirkwood's home and under his shade trees, until the military which had come to escort him and part of cabinet to the Charleston Hotel had formed a line. The ladies seeing this gathered in the piazza and the second story and fairly showered flowers upon him. Mr. Polk thereupon turned and acknowledged the compliment by removing his hat and bowing; the show a recognition they did not expect and which pleased them all the more. The ladies present on that occasion now living would take pleasure now in throwing flowers now on Mr. Polk's grave if they were near it.*[19]

Later, the Reverend Peschau delivered an address before the Historical and Scientific Society of North Carolina in which he voiced high praise of the much admired Mrs. Polk:

> Mrs. Polk enters, a tall, stately, graceful lady with beaming countenance and a dignified manner. She gives us a welcome that is so different from the stiff studied superiority of some would be greats that we are at a disadvantage and she must come to our rescue and she does. Such a clear mind, such choice, chaste language; the rapid flow of thought; her animation throughout; the quick wit; the rapid comprehending of what is said; and the ready answer. All interest us and charm us. Her knowledge of the times, her recollection of the past, how accurate! You are in the presence of a remarkable woman.[20]

In Sarah's last visit with the Rev. Peschau she spoke of her aware-
ness of the fact that she had grown old and of her lack of fear of growing old. "Yes, Peschau, I am growing old, I grow old willingly; I grow
old not unwillingly." Sarah recited: "The deepening shades, the fad-
ing light, / The chilling air, proclaim death's night, / But through the
gloom, light streams to me. / And I grow old quite willingly."[21]

Though Sarah apparently faced death willingly, the approach of
death for her was surrounded with some shadow and darkness.

A correspondent of the *Cincinnati Enquirer* wrote as follows: "It
is comparatively easy to describe the bloom and brilliancy of youth,
but to draw with a true touch the peculiar loveliness of old age is a far
more difficult task. A woman like Mrs. Polk is a revelation of the beau-
ties of old age. Gentle benevolence, broad reaching charity, ripe experience, and a cultivation of mind that extends beyond letters to come
to mankind shine through her conversation and ready memory, keen
wit and a store of reminiscences illuminate."[22]

Laura Holloway in her final observation on Mrs. Polk, wrote: "Surrounded with comforts and luxuries, and enjoying the companionship
of her relatives and friends, Mrs. Polk glides calmly down the vale of
years with the memory of a past all brightness, and the hope of a future
all peace. A lifetime imitation of a pure and useful standard of excellence has rewarded her with glorious fame and dwells among the friends
of her youth, honored and respected, trusted and beloved."[23]

A writer to Polk Place in the 1880s gave a word portrait of the former first lady that did little to enhance her image. She was described
as being above medium height, and seeming larger than she was. Her
weight was said to be exactly 135 pounds. "Her eyes are still large and
dark, her large firm nose still commanding. Usually her mouth was
slightly open like one about to speak, so that her upper teeth showed.
Some of those teeth were lacking, and others plainly artificial. Her dark
hair was hardly gray, but it may have been thinning, for she always wore
a bandeau of black and white crepe trimmed with black ribbons. Under
this, her hair was parted in the middle, and brought down in a clus-
ter of ringlets over each ear. The woman whose clothes had been the
admiration of Washington now kept to widow's black." She had like-
wise developed what the visitor called "a great deal of manner."[24]

Her financial position was secure, and was improved when in 1883
Congress passed a bill awarding a pension of $5,000 per year to the
widows of former presidents.[25]

A member of the staff of the *Nashville Banner* interviewed Mrs. Polk after the presidential election of 1884 when Grover Cleveland was elected. The interviewer wished Sarah to make a comparison between the present election and that of 1844 when her husband was made president. Sarah pleaded that too many years had elapsed for her to be able to recall all those events, for at the time of the election she and James were living in the small town of Columbia in Tennessee, where there were neither railroads nor telegraph systems.

However, when she was asked about the primary issues of 1844 she was able to recall that the primary issue then was the same as in 1884: tariffs. Another point of similarity that she was able to recall was that neither Cleveland nor Polk could have been made president without the vote of New York.

The reporter then brought up the question of the annexation of Texas and Sarah stated that the acquisition of Texas was indeed another major issue, and that there was much opposition to it. She stated that the contest was very heated.

Sarah continued to say that her increased age had reduced the excitement she had felt about such matters, though she had always taken a deep interest in state and national affairs. She added, "I regard the acquisition of Texas, and the results following the Mexican War, that is, the adding of California and New Mexico to the territory of the United States, as among the most important events in the history of this country, and that fact is becoming more and more apparent."[26]

Later in 1884 Senator John Sherman, brother of General William Sherman, came to visit Sarah. He reminded the former first lady that he and his wife had called on her at the White House when he and his wife were on their honeymoon. Sarah did not remember the senator, but she, always the gracious hostess, enjoyed a chat that lasted over an hour.[27]

The dear friends of Sarah's, Anson and Fanny Nelson, came to Polk Place on Christmas Eve 1885. Dicey, Sarah's servant and former slave, showed them into a room where Sarah sat writing. Sarah welcomed them in and told them that she was making some notes on what she could recall about the Mexican War. The notes were for someone who wished information on that conflict. Sarah received many requests for information on the past events that concerned the Polks. She told the Nelsons that she didn't turn out letters as fast as she once did, and some requests had to wait a long time for a response. She stated that most of these, however, were eventually answered.[28]

Sarah at that time was 82 years of age, and it is remarkable that she remained so active in keeping up her correspondence. This was one indication that she was bent on doing everything to preserve the memory of James Polk.[29]

George Bancroft, a noted historian and a good friend of the Polks, wrote to Colonel George Harris of his intention to visit Sarah. Colonel Harris asked Judge Lee, president of the Tennessee Historical Society, to arrange a welcoming committee, which duly accompanied Bancroft to the Maxwell House where he was to stay while in Nashville. At 86 years of age Bancroft was still active in mind and body. Later, an old friend, S. A. Cunningham, went with Bancroft to Polk Place. Bancroft rang the doorbell and Elias answered. When Sarah heard Bancroft's voice, she hastened to greet him. She stated her pleasure that Bancroft had come so far to visit her. After conversing a while, and as Bancroft was leaving, Sarah invited him to attend church with her on the following Sunday. He accepted the invitation and returned afterward to Polk Place for Sunday dinner. After the two had shared memories of the past, the historian told Sarah the true purpose of his visit. He was recording some history related to James Polk's administration, and he wished very much to have access to Polk's papers. Sarah responded that he was welcome to use any and all of James's papers which he needed, and promised to make them available.[30]

Prior to his visit to Nashville, Bancroft had written to Colonel Harris on April 8, 1887, from Washington, DC:

> If I feel well enough, I wish to run down before many days and see you all at Nashville. I want to do something for the memory of our friend James K. Polk. I think Mrs. Polk should not permit the papers of Mr. Polk to go out of her constant care for a moment; but I thought she might possibly allow me to take some of them to Washington with me and have them immediately copied and the originals returned to her. Speak with her about it, and tell me how she receives the suggestion. I propose to draw his character and especially the results of his administration; a full and just statement of them is of great interest for the whole nation, and you and I understand these things better than any others now alive.[31]

Mr. Bancroft was honored by so much attention while he was in Nashville that he did not have time to go through Polk's papers. Sarah, however, asked if he would like for her to send the papers to him in Washington. The historian expressed his pleasure at her generosity.

The *Saint Louis Republican* made note of the meeting between these two remarkable people:

> The meeting between the estimable lady who has been an ex-president's widow for thirty-eight years, and the venerable old gentleman who was first her husband's Secretary of Navy, and afterwards his Minister to the Court of Saint James was most courtly, candid, and happy. The days of the Polk administration were an age of courtly grace and retirement, and in the mellow splendor neither of them dreamed of the tragic four years with the following era of hard materialism which they have lived to see. Mr. Bancroft is well on toward ninety, and Mrs Polk close behind him.

After Bancroft left Nashville, Sarah filled a trunk with Polk's papers and had them shipped to him.[32]

As much as Sarah treasured the memory of her husband, and with her great desire that his record be preserved for posterity, it is remarkable that she would entrust his papers even to such a close friend as Bancroft.

What Bancroft received was a mass of Polk's notes and documents. He labored hard for a while, and even read back issues of the *Bay State Democrat* to improve his recall of the facts. Unfortunately, this project was not completed, except for a revision of an article in Appleton's *Encyclopedia* that called the Polk administration "perhaps the greatest in our national history, certainly one of the greatest." Bancroft had undertaken a great number of other projects related to American history, but he had been unable to complete them.[33]

Now at an advanced age, Bancroft, with his still active mind, presumed that he was still able to carry on as before. After he had become ambassador to the Court of St. James he had written many letters to President Polk. In his letters he rarely failed to include a closing note to Sarah. A characteristic ending was: "I beg my best regards to my great and good friend Mrs. Polk."[34]

At the Court of St. James, Bancroft and his wife observed, and were at times subject to, the snobbery of English polite society. Elizabeth Bancroft, George's second wife, who had the same exposure to the English upper crust, had informed Sarah Polk that the British elite were not really superior to their American counterparts. "We need not be ashamed of ourselves — our best bear a comparison with theirs."[35]

In October 1887 President Grover Cleveland embarked on a tour of the country to become better known to the electorate. This journey was known as the "swing around the circle." After visiting many cities the presidential party arrived at Belle Meade Farm, six miles outside of Nashville and one of the South's finest antebellum homes. Here the president was introduced to Sarah Polk, who was in her eighty-fifth year. Sarah insisted on rising to greet Cleveland. Dolley Madison had established the precedent for such action; she always rose to her feet when John Quincy Adams, as past president, entered a room where she was seated. Following the reception Mrs. Polk and Mrs. Cleveland talked of the concerns related to housekeeping in the White House.[36]

In November 1887 the Women's Christian Temperance Union met in Nashville. Frances Elizabeth Willard, former educator, was now the president of the organization. This noted lady, like all other important visitors to Nashville, felt that a call on the former first lady was requisite. Sarah told Mrs. Willard that she was much interested in the work of the Women's Christian Temperance Union and that if she were younger she would attend the meetings. During the conversation a large group from that organization called at Polk Place and were introduced to Sarah. The Nelsons, Fannie and Anson, recorded that soon after the meeting of the WCTU in Nashville, Sarah had several distinguished visitors, among whom were Valentine of Richmond, the famous sculptor, and Thomas Nelson Page, a noted U.S. author of several children's books. The latter was also a lecturer who gave readings from his stories of Southern life.[37]

On January 1, 1888, the Polks' sixtieth wedding anniversary, there were many callers at Polk Place. On January 3 Sarah's sister Susan died in Murfreesboro, leaving her as the only survivor of her immediate family. All of Susan's seven children had died earlier, and most of Sarah's relations and friends were gone. She expressed from time to time the wish that she too might, like her flowers, fade and disappear.[38]

On July 4, 1888, telegraph wires were strung to Polk Place. There were several invited guests to view this new marvel, which was placed on a table in the hallway. Sarah, as the eldest widow of a former president, was named to push the electric button that would set the apparatus in motion to open the Cincinnati Centennial Exposition. The exposition was commemorating the progress of Ohio and the central states during the last century. J. V. Rust and A. N. Stewart operated the wires for the Western Union Telegraph Company. At 11:15 A.M., the message came to Polk Place: "That upon this auspicious moment, when heaven has smiled upon this glorious northwestern territory, the same magnificent providence has spared to the citizens of the United States the wife of their revered President, James K. Polk."

Sarah replied, "Mrs. Polk acknowledges the courteous telegram just received, and hereby returns her thanks for the kind remembrances of her husband and herself upon this memorable occasion."

After sending her message, Sarah pressed the key to open the exposition. She received many congratulations, but she responded, "The honor which has been paid to me does not appeal to my pride. I recognize that it is a compliment to Mr. Polk, and it is one which I appreciate fully."[39]

In 1889 Sarah was visited by the Reverend H. M. Fields, who was passing through Nashville on his way to Washington where he meant to stay for a few days. By him Sarah sent her regards to Bancroft. Soon thereafter she received a letter from Fields:

> My dear Mrs. Polk,
>   Yesterday afternoon in company with my brother, Judge Fields, I paid a visit to Mr. Bancroft. We found him in his library looking somewhat aged but still bright with all his old fire. He was delighted to see us, and especially gratified to receive the message from you, to which he replied in the warmest manner saying that no one since Mrs. Washington had filled the place you occupied here with more perfect grace and dignity, and that you were remembered by the older residents with the utmost respect and affection. Nor was he less ardent in his praise of your husband, whose administration he pronounced one of the most brilliant in American history. This great distinction he said, was due to Mr. Polk himself; that he was not, like some Presidents, a mere figurehead of the government to be ruled by his cabinet, but that while he had indeed had a cabinet which comprised men of great ability, yet that he was the ablest of them all. He spoke of the great events of Mr. Polk's administration. The Mexican War, the acquisition of Texas, and of California, the latter bringing with it the great empire of the Pacific coast. All of this was very high praise to come from the historian of our country. After an hour's visit we could hardly tear ourselves from the eloquent old man, and as we departed he begged us to send to Mrs. Polk his most affectionate remembrances. To this I may add my own, and beg that you will now as then give a thought to one who considers it an honor to be permitted to call himself your friend.[40]

On Sarah's eighty-sixth birthday she received a letter from her dear friend, Bancroft, dated Washington, September 1889:

> My dear Mrs. Polk,
>   Your birthday returns, and your friends are happy in your continued health and enjoyment of life. As the oldest of them, as one who, if spared, will in a few years enter his ninetieth year, I congratulate you on your health and vigor. May the coming year be one of perfect health and happiness to you; you hold the affectionate regard of your country, and the esteem and best wishes of a nation ministered to your length of days better than all the efforts and care of the men of the healing arts can do. There is a constant refreshment of life in enjoying the highest esteem and regard of a free people, who elected your husband to be their chief, and who enabled him to fill his years of office with the greatest deeds. Live long, that you may more and more see the astonishing results of his administrative genius. Count me ever as one of the most earnest of your friends, perhaps the truest as the oldest of them all. Ever with affectionate regard. Your devoted friend, George Bancroft[41]

There were indications at this time, however, that Sarah was not as hale and hearty as Bancroft seemed to think. A former governor of Massachusetts calling on Sarah praised President Polk and pointed out the important achievements of his career. Sarah enjoyed the visit but told him in a pleasant way, "Had you not been accompanied by my relative, Mr. Childress, you would not have gained admittance to Polk Place. For my feebleness often prevents me from receiving visitors."[42]

Sarah had seen her great-niece, Saide Polk Fall, grow up at Polk Place to become a young woman. Saide was now engaged to be married. Sarah was asked by Fanny Nelson if she was excited about the upcoming wedding. Sarah replied, "Now, Fanny, an old woman doesn't get excited about things anymore. Saide wishes to get married at home and she says that if I am not able to witness the ceremony in the parlor, she will be married right here at my bedside." The marriage took place on May 12 and Sarah had recovered enough to witness the ceremony in the parlor.[43]

On January 17, 1891, George Bancroft died in his ninety-first year, and in March of the same year Sarah had a severe bout of pneumonia from which she recovered in a few weeks. After this she grew gradually more feeble and had difficulty in exerting herself even lightly. Getting in and out of a carriage put a great strain on her. In very hot

August weather, however, she rode out for three successive days. On the third day she returned to Polk Place to sit for awhile, talking in her usual fashion. But as she was returning to her room on the arm of a servant, her strength failed her. She appeared quite ill and lay down on her bed; she did not eat the meal on the table at her bedside. The next morning she seemed better, but soon it was evident that her strength was waning.[44]

There were periods of distress during the night, and the following day it was obvious that the end was near. Early the next morning her doctors were called to her bedside. One of the doctors informed the family that death was imminent. There was an emotional farewell spoken at the bedside by Sarah's family, and Sarah reaffirmed her faith and trust in God. Her last words were, "The Lord bless and keep thee and make his face to shine upon you and give you happiness, love and everlasting peace."[45]

The Reverend McNeilly was called for, but he did not arrive until after Mrs. Polk had died. Sally gave the good reverend instructions: "Aunt Sarah's body will rest here in her bedroom, where she has slept for forty-two years. The parlor is too large and lonely. She has requested that a white silk winding sheet be wrapped around her similar to the one that was used on Uncle Jim."[46]

After news of Sarah's death was announced, letters and telegrams poured in from all over the nation, and the general feeling was expressed in the next issue of *The American*:

> All the people of Tennessee grieve as the news goes forth that Mrs. James K. Polk is dead full of years and of honor, rich in devotion, and the tender affection of her household, and the deep universal esteem of Tennesseeans. The end of life came peacefully not as to one whom the infirmities of age and forgetfulness of friends has made weary of the world, but as to one blessed in all earthly surroundings and blessed in the sublime serenity of a Christian's faith. Conscious of the waning vitality which warned her of the approach of death, she has waited for the summons with cheerfulness and patience. It is needless to dwell upon the character of Mrs Polk. The intelligent mind undimmed to the end; and the unfailing gentleness which continued to the close, a loyal heart which cherished to the last the memory of the great man whose life was blessed with her constant devotion and faithful help. It is a positive blessing to this generation that this noble woman was spared to bring to bear upon it the beautiful characteristics and the splendid mental and heart training which were hers in a measure that can be said of few women. The South will for generations to come recall proudly her memory and point with profound pride to her career.[47]

Governor John Buchanan on August 14, 1891, wrote a letter directed to the family and friends of Mrs. James Polk:

> *On the part of Tennessee I desire to extend sympathy in this bereavement. I feel that not only the state, but the nation has sustained a loss in the death of so refined, so cultured, so noble a woman as Mrs. Polk, the widow of one of Tennessee's greatest, best beloved sons, and the nation's most exalted chieftain, James K. Polk. She has stood a peer among the women of the land, a perfect type of the gentle womanhood of the old south and her influence will live forever. The State of Tennessee will hold no spot more hallowed than that which has the honor to contain the remains of this distinguished son and his gentle wife, and will ever give all honors to their memory. With great respect, I beg leave to subscribe myself your obedient servant, John P. Buchanan, Governor of Tennessee*[48]

With all the laudatory comments made by friends of high station there is a conclusion to the story that seems strange. In Polk's will he had directed that Polk Place "be kept as a perpetual shrine. My beloved wife, Sarah Polk and myself have mutually agreed with each other, that at our respective deaths, it is desired that our bodies may be interred on the said premises ... the said house, lot and premises shall never pass into the hands of strangers ... nor shall any buildings or improvements be placed over the spot where our tomb may be." Despite a public demand that the terms of Polk's will must be honored, Tennessee refused to do so. The will was broken, the house was sold, and on September 18, 1893, James and Sarah Polk were reburied by the sovereign state of Tennessee, "with appropriate ceremonies" on Nashville's Capitol Hill.[49]

An inscription was put on the west side of the tomb:

Asleep in Jesus
Is Sarah Childress Polk
Wife of
James Knox Polk
Born in Rutherford County Tennessee
September 4, 1803
Died at Polk Place August 14, 1891
A noble woman, a devoted wife, a true friend, a sincere Christian [50]

On August 15, 1891, one day after the burial of Mrs. Polk, a letter was directed to Sarah's niece, Sally Fall, from Frances Elizabeth

Willard, president of the Women's Christian Temperance Union. The letter was full of noble thoughts and sentiments:

> *Dear friend — A noble Christian and a typical American lady of the old school has gone from this world, and a beloved aunt and household comrade has left your historic home. Seeing Mrs. Polk first in 1881, I omitted no opportunity to do so when in Nashville since then. The portrait at the White House placed there by American women, Northern and Southern, was a beautiful token of our renewed love and good understanding. The Christian example of Mrs. Polk at the executive mansion will brighten the annals of our country. These lines cannot express the full measure of appreciation and reverence that I have cherished for your illustrious aunt. Well might the church bells toll for one always loyal to our law, and the flags be placed at half mast for a patriot who dignified the name "American." May God's blessing be with you all who love her, and who have lost her out of your lives, is the prayers of Yours in the love of God and of Humanity.*
>
> *Frances E. Willard*[51]

In 1893 the bodies of James and Sarah Polk were taken from the mausoleum at Polk Place and placed in a tomb on the capitol grounds. On the tomb, prepared by A. O. P. Nicholson, is the epitaph:

"By his public policy he defined, established, and extended the boundaries of the country. He planted laws of the American union on the shores of the Pacific. His influence and his councils organized the national treasury on the principles of the Constitution, and to apply the rules of freedom to navigation, trade and industry."[52]

Notes

Chapter 1

1. Charles Sellers, *James K. Polk, Jacksonian*, 1:75.
2. Ibid.
3. Janie Lou Sparkman Claxton, *Eighty-Eight Years with Sarah Polk*, 13.
4. Ibid.
5. *James K. Polk*, Sellers, *Jacksonian*, 1:74.
6. Frances Griffin, *Less Time for Meddling, A History of Salem Academy and College, 1772–1866*, 5.
7. Anson and Fanny Nelson, *Memorials of Sarah Childress Polk*, 7.
8. Telephone conversation with Susan Taylor, Public Service Librarian, Salem College, Winston-Salem, NC.
9. General ledger entry, May 5, 1817, book 5, folio 13, Salem Academy, Winston-Salem, North Carolina.
10. Claxton, *Eighty-Eight Years*, 15.
11. Ibid.
12. Paul F. Boller, Jr., *Presidential Wives: An Anecdoctal History*, 89.
13. Claxton, *Eighty-Eight Years*, 15.
14. Griffin, *Less Time for* Meddling, 104.
15. Charles Sellers, *James K. Polk, Jacksonian*, 1:76.
16. Claxton, *Eighty-Eight Years*, 16.
17. Ibid.
18. Ibid., 17.

Chapter 2

1. Janie Lou Sparkman Claxton, *Eighty-Eight Years with Sarah Polk*, 212.
2. Sarah Agnes Wallace, "Letters of Mrs. James K. Polk to Her Husband," *Tennessee Historical Quarterly* 11, no. 2 (1952):181.
3. Paul F. Boller, Jr., *Presidential Wives: An Anecdoctal History*, 89.
4. Claxton, *Eighty-Eight Years*, 14.
5. Charles Sellers, *James K. Polk, Jacksonian*, 74.
6. Wallace, "Letters of Mrs. James K. Polk to Her Husband," 181.
7. Paul H. Bergeron, *The Presidency of James K. Polk*, 11.

8. Charles Sellers, *James K. Polk, Jacksonian*, 1:93.

9. Claxton, *Eighty-Eight Years*, 12.

10. Martha McBride Morrell, *"Young Hickory": The Life and Times of President James K. Polk*, 15.

11. Ibid., 25

12. Claxton, *Eighty-Eight Years*, 20.

13. Ibid.

14. Wallace, "Letters of Mrs. James K. Polk to Her Husband," 180.

15. Anson and Fanny Nelson, *Memorials of Sarah Childress Polk*, 16.

16. Diana Dixon Healy, *America's First Ladies*, 57.

17. Claxton, *Eighty-Eight Years*, 22.

18. Ibid.

19. Nelson, *Memorials*, 17.

20. Morrell, *"Young Hickory,"* 32.

21. Claxton, *Eighty-Eight Years*, 23.

22. Morrell, *"Young Hickory,"* 32.

23. Ibid., 33.

24. Ibid., 34.

25. Sellers, *James K. Polk, Jacksonian*, 1:94.

26. Ibid.

27. Ibid.

28. Ibid.

29. Claxton, *Eighty-Eight Years*, 28.

30. Sellers, *James K. Polk, Jacksonian*, 1:100.

31. Claxton, *Eighty-Eight Years*, 29.

32. Mary Ormsbee Whitton, *First First Ladies*, 204.

33. Sellers, *James K. Polk, Jacksonian*, 1:111.

34. Noel B. Gerson, *The Slender Reed*, 130.

35. Morrell, *"Young Hickory,"* 16–17.

36. Sellers, *James K. Polk, Jacksonian*, 1:40.

37. Robert M. Ikard, "Surgical Operations on James K. Polk," *Tennessee Historical Quarterly* 48, no.3 (1989):128–29.

38. Herbert Weaver, ed., *Correspondence of James K. Polk*, 1:69.

39. Ibid., 1:121–22.

40. Ikard, "Surgical Operations on James K. Polk," 128–29.

41. Whitton, *First First Ladies*, 204.

42. Ibid.

43. Ibid.

44. Ibid.

45. Nelson, *Memorials*, 31.

46. Sellers, *James K. Polk, Jacksonian*, 1:111.

47. Claxton, *Eighty-Eight Years*, 32.

48. Sellers, *James K. Polk, Jacksonian*, 1:114.

49. Ibid., 117.

50. Claxton, *Eighty-Eight Years*, 13.

Chapter 3

1. Charles Sellers, *James K. Polk, Jacksonian*, 1:132.
2. Herbert Weaver, ed., *Correspondence of James K. Polk*, 1:269.
3. Anson and Fanny Nelson, *Memorials of Sarah Childress Polk*, 39.
4. Ibid., 40.
5. Martha McBride Morrell, *"Young Hickory": The Life and Times of President James K. Polk*, 51.
6. Sellers, *James K. Polk, Jacksonian*, 1:150.
7. Morrell, *"Young Hickory,"* 54.
8. Sellers, *James K. Polk, Jacksonian*, 1:143.
9. Morrell, *"Young Hickory,"* 54.
10. Sellers, *James K. Polk, Jacksonian*, 1:384.
11. Weaver, ed. *Correspondence*, 1:398.
12. Ibid., 1:426.
13. Janie Lou Sparkman Claxton, *Eighty-Eight Years with Sarah Polk*, 41.
14. Nelson, *Memorials,* 46.
15. Sellers, *James K. Polk, Jacksonian*, 1:184.
16. Ibid.
17. Ibid.
18. Claxton, *Eighty-Eight Years,* 31.
19. Ibid., 39.
20. Ibid., 31.
21. Morrell, *"Young Hickory,"* 54.
22. J. J. Farrell, *James K. Polk, 1795–1849*, 4.
23. Sellers, *James K. Polk, Jacksonian*, 1:232.
24. Ibid., 248.
25. Morrell, Mary Ormsbee *"Young Hickory,"* 94.
26. Whitton, *First First Ladies*, 207.
27. Weaver, ed., *Correspondence*, 1:271.
28. Ibid., 1:351.
29. Ibid., 1:402.
30. Claxton, *Eighty-Eight Years,* 45.
31. Anthony Carl Sferrazza, *First Ladies: A Saga of the Presidents' Wives and Their Power*, 35.
32. Nelson, *Memorials,* 49.
33. Morrell, *"Young Hickory,"* 100.
34. Sellers, *James K. Polk, Jacksonian*, 1:331.
35. Nelson, *Memorials,* 53.
36. Morrell, *"Young Hickory,"* 143.
37. Paul F. Boller, Jr., *Presidential Wives: An Anecdoctal History*, 89.
38. Weaver, ed., *Correspondence*, 5:126.
39. Eugene Irving McCormac, *James K. Polk: A Political Biography*, 158.

40. Ibid., 159.
41. Morrell, "*Young Hickory*," 149.
42. Alfred Laland Crabb, *Nashville, Personality of a City*, 117.

Chapter 4

1. Sarah Agnes Wallace, "Letters of Mrs. James K. Polk to Her Husband," *Tennessee Historical Quarterly* 11, no. 2 (1952):182–83.
2. Herbert, Weaver, ed., *Correspondence of James K. Polk*, 5:557.
3. Wallace, "Letters of Mrs. James K. Polk to Her Husband," 182–83.
4. Weaver, ed., *Correspondence*, 5:665.
5. Weaver, ed., *Correspondence*, 5:674.
6. Ibid., 5:675.
7. Paul H. Bergeron, *The Presidency of James K. Polk*, 2.
8. Ibid., 14.
9. Charles A. McCoy, *Polk and the Presidency*, 37.
10. Ibid.
11. Anthony Carl Sferrazza, *First Ladies: A Saga of the Presidents' Wives and Their Power*, 135.
12. Janie Lou Sparkman Claxton, *Eighty-Eight Years with Sarah Polk*, 57.
13. Martha McBride Morrell, "*Young Hickory*": *The Life and Times of President James K. Polk*, 205.
14. Sferrazza, *First Ladies*, 135.
15. Ibid.
16. Claxton, *Eighty-Eight Years*, 57.
17. Ibid.
18. Jane Burt McConnell, *Our First Ladies*, 125.
19. Claxton, *Eighty-Eight Years*, 67.
20. Ibid., 61.
21. Morrell, "*Young Hickory*," 234.
22. Claxton, *Eighty-Eight Years*, 62.
23. Morrell, "*Young Hickory*," 241.
24. Anson and Fanny Nelson, *Memorials of Sarah Childress Polk*, 86.
25. Ibid.
26. Ibid.
27. Charles Sellers, *James K. Polk, Continentalist*, 2:206.
28. Ibid.
29. Morrell, "*Young Hickory*," 241.
30. Nelson, *Memorials*, 87.
31. Ibid., 87–88.
32. Morrell, "*Young Hickory*," 248.
33. Nelson, *Memorials*, 88.
34. Peter Hay, *All the Presidents' Ladies*, 180.
35. Kathleen Prindeville, *First Ladies*, 111.

36. Ibid., 122.
37. Marianne Means, *The Woman in the White House*, 79.
38. Sol Barzman, *The First Ladies*, 170.
39. Paul F. Boller, Jr., *Presidential Wives: In the White House*, 88.
40. Means, *The Woman*, 79.
41. Nelson, *Memorials*, 91.
42. Sellers, *An Anecdotal History, Polk, Continentalist*, 2:307.
43. William Seale, *The President's House*, 1:257.
44. Nelson, *Memorials*, 91.
45. Sferrazza, *First Ladies*, 138.
46. Ibid.

Chapter 5

1. Anson and Fanny Nelson, *Memorials of Sarah Childress Polk*, 112.
2. Amy Lafolette Jensen, *The White House and Its Thirty-Five Families*, 69.
3. Marianne Means, *The Woman in the White House*, 78.
4. Paul F. Boller, Jr., *Presidential Wives: An Anecdoctal History,* 37.
5. Janie Lou Sparkman Claxton, *Eighty-Eight Years with Sarah Polk*, 70.
6. Bess Furman, *White House Profile: Sarah Childress Polk*, 137.
7. William Seale, *The President's House*, 1:265.
8. Ibid.
9. Boller, *Presidential Wives,* 93.
10. Charles A. McCoy, *Polk and the Presidency*, 57.
11. Paul H. Bergeron, *The Presidency of James K. Polk*, 152.
12. Milo Milton Quaife, ed., *The Diary of James K. Polk During His Presidency*, 1:107.
13. Hugh Brogan and Charles Morley, *American Presidential Families*, 380.
14. Martha McBride Morrell, *"Young Hickory": The Life and Times of President James K. Polk*, 94.
15. Webb Garrison, *White House Tales*, 160.
16. Boller, *Presidential Wives*, 91.
17. Margaret Truman, *First Ladies*, 102–3.
18. John R. Bumgarner, *The Health of the Presidents*, 181.
19. Kenneth R. Crispell and Carlos E. Gomez, *Hidden Illness in the White House*, 189.
20. Anthony Carl Sferrazza, *First Ladies: A Saga of the Presidents' Wives and Their Power*, 140.
21. Jack Shepherd, *The Adams Chronicles: Four Generations of Greatness*, 76.
22. Means, *The Woman in the White House*, 80.
23. Ibid., 81.

24. Lately Thomas, *The First President Johnson: The Three Lives of the Seventeenth President of the United States of America*, 66
25. Ibid.
26. Anne Furor Scott, *The Southern Lady: From Pedestal to Politics, 1830 to 1930*, 17.
27. Sferrazza, *First* Ladies, 141.
28. Betty Boyd Caroli, *First Ladies*, 61.
29. Charles Sellers, *James K. Polk, Jacksonian*, 1:246.
30. Herbert Weaver, ed., *Correspondence of James K. Polk*, 2:516.
31. Ibid., 1:72.
32. Ibid., 6:356.
33. Elbert B. Smith, *The Presidency of James Buchanan*, 13.
34. Claxton, *Eighty-Eight Years*, 80.
35. Seale, *The President's House*, 1:26.
36. Mary Ormsbee Whitton, *These Were the Women*, 167.
37. Seale, *The President's House*, 1:261.
38. Claxton, *Eighty-Eight Years*, 71.
39. Quaife, *Diary of James K. Polk*, 1:37.
40. Ibid., 1:35.
41. Claxton, *Eighty-Eight Years*, 72.
42. Ibid., 73.
43. Philip Shriver Kline, *President James Buchanan*, 275.

Chapter 6

1. Janie Lou Sparkman Claxton, *Eighty-Eight Years with Sarah Polk*, 69.
2. Ibid., 68.
3. Paul H. Bergeron, *The Presidency of James K. Polk*, 221.
4. Samuel Elliot Morrison, *The Oxford History of the American People*, 445.
5. Ibid.
6. Ibid., 451.
7. Bergeron, *The Presidency of James K. Polk*, 220–21.
8. John William Ward, *Andrew Jackson, Symbol for an Age*, 147.
9. Ibid.
10. Ibid., 220.
11. Reinhold Niebuhr, *The Irony of American History*, 47.
12. Frederick Alfred Merk, *Manifest Destiny*, 24.
13. Ibid.
14. Ibid.
15. Charles Sellers, *James K. Polk, Continentalist*, 2:214.
16. Sol Barzman, *The First Ladies*, 107.
17. Mary Ormsbee Whitton, *First First Ladies*, 209.
18. Ibid.

19. Roy Basler, ed., *Abraham Lincoln: His Speeches and Writings*, 199–200.
20. William Seale, *The President's House*, 1:254.
21. Anthony Carl Sferrazza, *First Ladies: A Saga of the Presidents' Wives and Their Power*, 141.
22. Seale, *The President's House*, 1:254.
23. Sferrazza, *First Ladies*, 141.
24. Seale, *The President's House*, 1:262.
25. Claxton, *Eight-Eight Years*, 81.
26. Diana Dixon Healy, *America's First Ladies*, 57.
27. Kathleen Prindeville, *First Ladies*, 112.
28. Martha McBride Morrell, *"Young Hickory": The Life and Times of President James K. Polk*, 273.
29. Sellers, *James K. Polk, Continentalist*, 2:481.
30. Ibid.
31. Milo Milton Quaife, ed., *Diary of James K. Polk During His Presidency*, 3:11.
32. Quaife, *Diary of James K. Polk*, 3:92–93.
33. Morrell, *"Young Hickory,"* 279.
34. Paul F. Boller, Jr., *Presidential Wives: An Anecdoctal History*, 100.
35. Margaret Truman, *First Ladies*, 99.
36. Barzman, *The First Ladies*, 106.
37. Hugh Brogan and Charles Morley, *American Presidential Families*, 380.
38. Robert E. Hales, Stuart Yudofsky, and John A. Talbot, *Textbook of Psychiatry*, 707.
39. Quaife, *Diary of James K. Polk*, 3:3.
40. Ibid., 3:9.
41. John R. Bumgarner, *The Health of the Presidents*, 4.
42. Quaife, *Diary of James K. Polk*, 3:19.
43. Claxton, *Eighty-Eight Years*, 88.
44. Ibid., 89.
45. William D. Snider, *Light on the Hill. A History of the University of North Carolina at Chapel Hill*, 62.
46. Claxton, *Eighty-Eight Years*, 90.
47. Ibid., 91.
48. Anson and Fanny Nelson, *Memoirs of Sarah Childress Polk*, 105.
49. Morrell, *"Young Hickory,"* 303.
50. Claxton, *Eighty-Eight Years*, 94.
51. Ibid.

Chapter 7

1. Anson and Fanny Nelson, *Memorials of Sarah Childress Polk*, 109.
2. Milo Milton Quaife, ed., *Diary of James K. Polk During His Presidency*, 3:83–84.

3. Ibid., 3:187–88.

4. Ibid., 3:195.

5. Ibid.

6. Janie Lou Sparkman Claxton, *Eighty-Eight Years with Sarah Polk*, 95.

7. Paul F. Boller, Jr., *Presidential Wives: An Anecdoctal History*, 94.

8. Betty Boyd Caroli, *First Ladies*, 66.

9. Ibid.

10. Nelson, *Memorials*, 116.

11. Ibid., 117.

12. Quaife, *Diary of James K. Polk*, 3:326.

13. Nelson, *Memorials*, 116.

14. Paul H. Bergeron, *The Presidency of James K. Polk*, 232.

15. Charles Sellers, *James K. Polk, Jacksonian*, 1:459.

16. Bergeron, *The Presidency of James K. Polk*, 232.

17. Sellers, *James K. Polk, Jacksonian*, 1:184.

18. Bergeron, *The Presidency of James K. Polk*, 238.

19. Ibid.

20. Ibid.

21. Ibid., 242.

22. Claxton, *Eighty-Eight Years*, 104.

23. Bergeron, *The Presidency of James K. Polk*, 239.

24. Nelson, *Memorials*, 118.

25. Bergeron, *The Presidency of James K. Polk*, 244.

26. Nelson, *Memorials*, 120.

27. Claxton, *Eighty-Eight Years*, 116.

28. Bill Adler, *Presidential Wit*, 37.

29. Martha McBride Morrell, *"Young Hickory": The Life and Times of President James K. Polk*, 306.

30. Quaife, *Diary of James K. Polk*, 4:377.

31. Bergeron, *The Presidency of James K. Polk*, 241.

32. Morrell, *"Young Hickory,"* 348.

33. Claxton, *Eighty-Eight Years*, 122–23.

34. Morrell, *"Young Hickory,"* 349.

35. Quaife, *Diary of James K. Polk*, 4:397.

36. Ibid., 4:398.

37. Ibid., 4:400.

38. Claxton, *Eighty-Eight Years*, 124.

Chapter 8

1. Martha McBride Morrell, *"Young Hickory": The Life and Times of President James K. Polk*, 350–51.

2. Ibid., 351.

3. Milo Milton Quaife, ed., *Diary of James K. Polk During His Presidency*, 3:412–13.

4. Ibid., 3:413.
5. Anson and Fanny Nelson, *Memorials of Sarah Childress Polk*, 137.
6. Ibid.
7. Quaife, *Diary of James K. Polk*, 4:417.
8. Nelson, *Memorials*, 138.
9. Morrell, *"Young Hickory,"* 356.
10. Quaife, *Diary of James K. Polk*, 4:425.
11. Thomas Perkins Abernathy, *From Frontier to Plantation in Tennessee*, 283.
12. Ibid.
13. Ibid., 282.
14. Morrell, *"Young Hickory,"* 357.
15. Ibid.
16. John R. Bumgarner, *The Health of the Presidents*, 70.
17. Paul H. Bergeron, *The Presidency of James K. Polk*, 260.
18. Earl Irving West, "Religious Beliefs of James K. Polk," *Tennessee Historical Quarterly* 26, no. 4 (1967): 369.
19. Nelson, *Memorials*, 150.
20. Mary Ormsbee Whitton, *First First Ladies*, 211.
21. Morrell, *"Young Hickory,"* 363.
22. Nelson, *Memorials*, 151.
23. Janie Lou Sparkman Claxton, *Eighty-Eight Years with Sarah Polk*, 136.
24. Ibid., 151.
25. Jane Burt McConnell, *Our First Ladies*, 129.
26. Claxton, *Eighty-Eight Years*, 137.

Chapter 9

1. Mary Ormsbee Whitton, *First First Ladies*, 216.
2. John Spencer Bassett, *The Southern Plantation Overseer*, 178.
3. Ibid., 179.
4. Ibid., 181.
5. Whitton, *First First Ladies*, 212.
6. Ibid., 215.
7. Anson and Fanny Nelson, *Memorials of Sarah Childress Polk*, 162.
8. Janie Lou Sparkman Claxton, *Eighty-Eight Years with Sarah Polk*, 142.
9. Nelson, *Memorials*, 163.
10. Ibid., 164.
11. Laura Carter Holloway, *Ladies of the White House*, 461.
12. Ibid., 463.
13. Claxton, *Eighty-Eight Years*, 141.
14. Whitton, *First First Ladies*, 216.

15. Claxton, *Eighty-Eight Years*, 143.
16. Ibid.
17. Nelson, *Memorials*, 166.
18. Whitton, *First First Ladies*, 214.
19. Bassett, *The Southern Plantation Overseer*, 188.
20. Ibid., 162.
21. Ibid., 324.
22. Nathaniel Weyl and Marina William, *Slavery and the Negro*, 126.
23. Ibid.
24. Claxton, *Eighty-Eight Years*, 145.
25. Bassett, *The Southern Plantation Overseer*, 197.
26. Ibid., 199.
27. Ibid., 200.

Chapter 10

1. Janie Lou Sparkman Claxton, *Eighty-Eight Years with Sarah Polk*, 143.
2. William B. Hesseltine, ed., *Autobiography and Letters of J. G. M. Ramsey, M.D.*, 240–41.
3. Claxton, *Eighty-Eight Years*, 144.
4. Ibid., 145.
5. Ibid., 146.
6. Philip Shriver Kline, *President James Buchanan*, 161.
7. Ibid., 252.
8. Ibid., 340.
9. Jane Burt McConnell, *Our First Ladies*, 128.
10. John Spencer Bassett, *The Southern Plantation Overseer*, 211.
11. Dr. Richard Bardolph, private communication.
12. Bassett, *The Southern Plantation Overseer*, 212.
13. Claxton, *Eighty-Eight Years*, 148.
14. Laura Carter Holloway, *Ladies of the White House*, 460.
15. Ibid., 461.
16. Anson and Fanny Nelson, *Memorials of Sarah Childress Polk*, 165.
17. Bassett, *The Southern Plantation Overseer*, 220.
18. Henry McRaven, *Nashville, Athens of the South*, 94.
19. Ibid.
20. Bruce Catton, *Terrible Swift Sword*, 161.
21. Ibid.
22. Nelson, *Memorials*, 173.
23. Claxton, *Eighty-Eight Years*, 155.
24. Ibid., 171.
25. Ibid., 156.
26. Christopher Chancellor, ed., *Henry Yates Thompson: An Englishman on the Civil War*, 24.

27. Elvira E. Powers, *Hospital Pencillings*, 30.
28. Claxton, *Eighty-Eight Years*, 153.
29. Powers, *Pencillings*, 99.
30. Ibid., 106.
31. Ibid.
32. Shelby Foote, *The Civil War*, 3:672.
33. Winston Groome, *Shrouds of Glory*, 207.
34. Ibid., *Shrouds of Glory*, 212.
35. Stanley J. Folmsbee, Robert E. Corlew, and Enoch L. Mitchell, *Tennessee: A Short History*, 339.
36. Alfred Laland Crabb, *Nashville, Personality of a City*, 66.
37. Ibid.

Chapter 11

1. Alfred Laland Crabb, *Nashville, Personality of a City*, 66.
2. Janie Lou Sparkman Claxton, *Eighty-Eight Years with Sarah Polk*, 156.
3. Henry McRaven, *Nashville: Athens of the South*, 100.
4. Ibid.
5. Laura Carter Holloway, *Ladies of the White House*, 462.
6. Claxton, *Eighty-Eight Years*, 162.
7. Anson and Fanny Nelson, *Memorials of Sarah Childress Polk*, 185.
8. Holloway, *Ladies of the White House*, 463.
9. Nelson, *Memorials*, 187.
10. Harry Barnard, *Rutherford B. Hayes and His America*, 149.
11. Emily Apt Gere, *First Lady: The Life of Lucy Webb Hayes*, 144.
12. Ibid., 145.
13. Ibid., 250.
14. McRaven, *Nashville*, 124.
15. Claxton, *Eighty-Eight Years*, 164.
16. Sol Barzman, *The First Ladies*, 109.
17. Holloway, *Ladies of the White House*, 421.
18. Nelson, *Memorials*, 189.
19. Ibid., 191.
20. Ibid., 192.
21. Ibid., 193.
22. Ibid., 196.
23. Holloway, *Ladies of the White House*, 464.
24. Mary Ormsbee Whitton, *First First Ladies*, 217.
25. Claxton, *Eighty-Eight Years*, 171.
26. Nelson, *Memorials*, 199.
27. Claxton, *Eighty-Eight Years*, 175.
28. Ibid., 177.

29. Ibid., 175.
30. Ibid., 177.
31. M. A. Oswulf Howe, *The Life and Letters of George Bancroft*, 2:312.
32. Claxton, *Eighty-Eight Years*, 180.
33. Lillian Handlin, *George Bancroft, the Intellectual as Democrat*, 341.
34. Howe, *The Life and Letters*, 2:29.
35. Handlin, *George Bancroft*, 2:28.
36. Dennis Tilden Lynch, *Grover Cleveland: A Man Four-Square*, 347.
37. Nelson, *Memorials*, 216.
38. Claxton, *Eighty-Eight Years*, 188.
39. Ibid., 190.
40. Nelson, *Memorials*, 225.
41. Claxton, *Eighty-Eight Years*, 196.
42. Ibid., 194.
43. Ibid., 200.
44. Nelson, *Memorials*, 273.
45. Ibid., 275.
46. Claxton, *Eighty-Eight Years*, 202.
47. Nelson, *Memorials*, 277.
48. Claxton, *Eighty-Eight Years*, 203.
49. Barzman, *The First Ladies*, 109.
50. Claxton, *Eighty-Eight Years*, 207.
51. Nelson, *Memorials*, 284.
52. Eugene Irving McCormac, *James K. Polk: A Political Biography*, 722.

Bibliography

Books

Abernathy, Thomas Perkins. *From Frontier to Plantation in Tennessee*. Chapel Hill: University of North Carolina Press, 1932.

Adler, Bill. *Presidential Wit*. New York: Trident, 1968.

Anthony, Catherine. *Dolley Madison: Her Life and Times*. Garden City, NJ: Doubleday, 1949.

Barnard, Harry. *Rutherford B. Hayes and His America*. Indianapolis: Bobbs-Merrill, 1954.

Barzman, Sol. *The First Ladies*. New York: Cowles Book, Inc., 1970.

Basler, Roy, ed. *Abraham Lincoln: His Speeches and Writings*. Cleveland, NY: World Publishing, 1946.

Bassett, John Spencer. *The Southern Plantation Overseer*. Printed for Smith College, Northampton, MA, 1825.

Bergeron, Paul H. *The Presidency of James K. Polk*. Lawrence: University Press of Kansas, 1987.

Boller, Paul F., Jr. *Presidential Wives: An Anecdotal History*. New York: Oxford University Press, 1988.

Brogan, Hugh, and Charles Morley. *American Presidential Families*. New York: Macmillan, 1993.

Buell, Augustus C. *History of Andrew Jackson*, Vol. 1. New York: Charles Scribner's Sons, 1904.

Bumgarner, John R. *The Health of the Presidents*. Jefferson, NC: McFarland, 1994.

Caroli, Betty Boyd. *First Ladies*. New York: Oxford University Press, 1987.

Catton, Bruce. *Terrible Swift Sword*. Garden City, NJ: Doubleday, 1963.

Chancellor, Christopher, ed. *Henry Yates Thompson: An Englishman on the Civil War*. London: Sidgewick and Jackson, 1871.

Claxton, Janie Lou Sparkman. *Eighty-Eight Years with Sarah Polk*. New York: Vantage, 1972.

Coit, Margaret, *J.C. Calhoun: American Portrait*. Boston: Houghton Mifflin, 1858.

Crabb, Alfred Laland. *Nashville, Personality of a City*. New York: Bobbs and Merrill, 1960.

Crispell, Kenneth R., and Carlos E. Gomez. *Hidden Illness in the White House*. Durham, NC: Duke University Press, 1988.

Farrell, J. J., *James K. Polk, 1795–1849*. Dobbs Ferry, NY: Oceana, 1970.
Folmsbee, Stanley J., Robert E. Corlew, and Enoch L. Mitchell. *Tennessee: A Short History*. Knoxville: University of Tennessee Press, 1969.
Foote, Shelby. *The Civil War, vol. 3*. New York: Random House, 1974.
Furman, Bess. *White House Profile: Sarah Childress Polk*. Indianapolis: Bobbs-Merrill, 1951.
Garrison, Webb. *White House Tales*. Nashville, TN: Rutledge Hill, 1989.
Gere, Emily Apt. *First Lady: The Life of Lucy Webb Hayes*. Kent, OH: Kent State University Press, 1984.
Gerson, Noel B. *The Slender Reed: A Biographical Novel of James K. Polk*. New York: Doubleday, 1965.
Griffin, Frances. *Less Time for Meddling: A History of Salem Academy and College, 1772–1866*. Winston-Salem, NC: John F. Blair, 1979.
Groome, Winston. *Shrouds of Glory*. New York: Atlantic Monthly, 1995.
Hales, Robert E., Stuart Yudofsky, and John A. Talbot, *Textbook of Psychiatry*. Washington, DC: American Psychiatric Press, 1994.
Handlin, Lillian. *George Bancroft, the Intellectual as Democrat*. New York: Harper and Row, 1986.
Hay, Peter. *All the Presidents' Ladies*. New York: Viking, 1988.
Healy, Diana Dixon. *America's First Ladies*. New York: Atheneum, 1988.
Hesseltine, William B., ed. *Autobiography and Letters of J. G.M. Ramsey, M.D.* (1886). Nashville: Tennessee Historical Commission, 1954.
Holloway, Laura Carter. *Ladies of the White House*. San Francisco: H. H. Bancroft, 1870.
Howe, M. A. Oswulf. *The Life and Letters of George Bancroft, vol 2*. New York: Charles Scribner's Son, 1908.
Jensen, Amy LaFolette. *The White House and Its Thirty-Five Families*. New York: McGraw-Hill, 1966.
Kline, Philip Shriver. *President James Buchanan*. University Park: Pennsylvania State University Press, 1962.
Lynch, Dennis Tilden. *Grover Cleveland: A Man Four-Square*. New York: H. Liveright, 1932.
McConnell, Jane Burt. *Our First Ladies*. New York: Thomas Crowell, 1961.
McCormac, Eugene Irving. *James K. Polk: A Political Biography*. New York: Russell and Russell, 1965.
McCoy, Charles A. *Polk and the Presidency*. Austin: University of Texas Press, 1960.
McRaven, Henry. *Nashville: Athens of the South*. Chapel Hill, NC: Scheer and Jarvis, 1949.
Marx, Rudolph. *The Health of the Presidents*. New York: G. P. Putnam, 1960.
Means, Marianne. *The Woman in the White House*. New York: Random House, 1963.
Merk, Frederick Alfred. *Manifest Destiny*. New York: Alfred A. Knopf, 1963.
Morison, Samuel Eliot. *The Oxford History of the American People*. New York: Oxford University Press, 1965.

Morrell, Martha McBride. *"Young Hickory": The Life and Times of President James K. Polk.* New York: G. P. Dutton, 1941.

Nelson, Anson, and Fanny Nelson. *Memorials of Sarah Childress Polk.* New York: Anson D. F. Randolph, 1892.

Niebuhr, Reinhold. *The Irony of American History.* New York: Charles Scribner's Sons, 1952.

Powers, Elvira E. *Hospital Pencillings.* Chicago: New Covenant, 1846.

Prindeville, Kathleen. *First Ladies.* New York: Macmillan, 1941

Quaife, Milo Milton, ed. *The Diary of James K. Polk During His Presidency,* vols. 1, 3, 4. Chicago: Chicago Historical Society, 1910.

Scott, Anne Furor. *The Southern Lady, from Pedestal to Politics, 1830 to 1930.* Chicago: University of Chicago Press, 1970.

Seale, William. *The President's House: A History.* Vol. 1. Washington, DC: White House Historical Association and Harry N. Abrams, 1986

_____. *James K. Polk, Jacksonian, vol 1.* Princeton, NJ: Princeton University Press, 1957.

Sellers, Charles. *James K. Polk, Continentalist.* Princeton, NJ: Princeton University Press, 1966.

Sferrazza, Anthony Carl. *First Ladies: A Saga of the Presidents' Wives and Their Power.* New York: William Morrow, 1990.

Shepherd, Jack. *The Adams Chronicles: Four Generations of Greatness.* Boston: Little, Brown, 1975.

Smith, Elbert B. *The Presidency of James Buchanan.* Lawrence: University of Kansas Press, 1977.

Snider, William D. *Light on the Hill. A History of the University of North Carolina at Chapel Hill.* Chapel Hill: University of North Carolina Press, 1992.

Thomas, Lately. *The First President Johnson: The Three Lives of the Seventeenth President of the United States of America.* New York: William Morrow, 1968.

Truman, Margaret. *First Ladies.* New York: Random House, 1963.

Ward, John William. *Andrew Jackson, Symbol for an Age.* London: Oxford University Press, 1955.

Weaver, Herbert, ed. *Correspondence of James K. Polk,* vols. 1, 2, 5, 6, Nashville: Vanderbilt University Press, 1969.

Weyl, Nathaniel, and Marina Williams. *Slavery and the Negro.* New Rochelle, NY: Arlington House, 1971.

Whitton, Mary Ormsbee. *First First Ladies.* New York: Hastings House, 1948.

_____. *These Were the Women.* New York: Hastings House, 1954.

Journals

Ikard, Robert M. "Surgical Operations on James K. Polk." *Tennessee Historical Quarterly,* 48, no. 3:128–129.

Wallace, Sarah Agnes. "Letters of Mrs. James K. Polk to Her Husband." *Tennessee Historical Quarterly,* 11, no. 2 (1952):180–83.
West, Earl Irving. "Religious Beliefs of James K. Polk." *Tennessee Historical Quarterly,* 26, no. 4 (1967).
Whitney, David C. *The American Presidents.* New York: Prentice Hall, 1990.

Miscellaneous

Ledger entry, May 5, 1817, book 5, folio 12, Salem Academy, Winston-Salem, NC.
Private communication with Dr. Richard Bardolph.
Telephone conversation with Susan Taylor, Public Service Librarian, Salem College, Winston-Salem, NC.

Index

174 INDEX

Smallpox 34, 137; vaccine 34
Smith, Thomas 21
Smithland 108
Smithwell, South Carolina 103
Snakeroot, White 15
Spas in Virginia and Pennsylvania 95
Speaker of the House 39, 40, 41, 45
Spencer, The Reverend 98
Spring Hill, Tennessee 109
Stagecoach lines 111
Stanton, Elizabeth Cady 94
Stephen, Anne 100
Stevenson, Vernon K. 56, 92, 127
Stewart, A. N. 148
Story, Joseph D. 45, 46, 74
Sullivan, John L. 79
Sullivan County, Tennessee 45
Sully, Mr. 88
Sumner, Charles 99
Sumner County, Tennessee 15
Supreme Court 45; judges of 74
Swain, D. Y. 88
Swann's Hotel 102, 103

Taft, Helen 67
Taney, Roger B. 39, 58
Tariffs 145; reduction in 76
Taswell, Littleton W. 32
Taylor, Zachary 85, 101, 102
Tea boycott 68
Telegram 149
Telegraph wires 148
Telephone 142
Temperance movement 73, 141
Tennessee: capital moved 46; capitol 47; His-
 torical Society 121, 146; House of Represen-
 tatives 27
Teresa (seamstress, maid) 64
Texas 55, 74; annexation of 53, 54, 56, 74,
 76, 78, 79, 145, 149
Thomaston, Georgia 104
Thompson, Henry Yates 134
Tornado 126
Tuberculosis 43
Tyler, John 60, 141; administration 56
Tyler, Mrs. John 62
Typhoid 15

U.S. Bank 35, 39, 42
U.S. Cabinet 74, 80, 83, 93, 101
U.S. House of Representatives 27
U.S. Military Academy 98
Union 131; officers 133; troops 132, 136
United Brethren 17
University of Louisville 27
University of Nashville 111
University of North Carolina at Chapel Hill
 17, 20, 38, 88
University of the South at Sewanee, Tennessee
 65

Valentine of Richmond (sculptor) 148
Van Buren, John 65, 66
Van Buren, Martin 40, 46, 49, 53, 65, 66, 70,
 95
Vera Cruz 80
Virginia Theological Seminary 65

Walker J. Knox (nephew to James) 23, 56, 88
Walker, Colonel James H. 92
Walker, Mrs. James H. 92
Walker, Robert J. 81
Walker, Samuel P. 31, 49, 94
Wallace, Sarah Agnes 23
Washington, D.C. 27, 28, 29, 32, 34, 37, 38,
 43, 56, 90, 134; society 31
Washington, President George 64
Washington County, Tennessee 45
Washington Monument 99
Washington Post 100
Watson, Colonel 105
Wee-No-Shick (Winnebago chief) 121
West Point 65, 98, 124
Western Military Institute 133
Western Union Telegraph Company 148
Wheeling, West Virginia 32, 43, 56
Whigs 46, 52, 55, 96, 101, 141
White, Hugh 28, 31, 32
White House 34, 60, 61, 69, 72, 76, 81, 140;
 Blue Room 75; housekeeping in 69, 148; lit
 by gas 88, 89; papers 59; party 63, 75, 99,
 101; West Room 75
Whitefield's Hotel 102
Whitfield, Virginia 38
Whitsett, Eliash (nephew to Sarah) 133, 137
Whitsett, John, Jr. (nephew to Sarah) 133, 137
Whittington, The Reverend 98
Whitton, Mary Ormsbee 28
Wilkinson, Commodore 84
Willamette Valley 76
Willard, Frances Elizabeth 148, 152, 153
Williams, Mrs. 83
Williamson's Hotel 29
Wilmington, North Carolina 102
Wilson, Edith Galt 15, 67
Wilson, Woodrow 67
Women's Christian Temperance Union 148,
 153
Women: education at subscription schools 16;
 rights 68, 94; role of 70
Woodberry Levi 32, 34, 36, 74, 90
Wormsley, John C. 29
Worth, General 80
Wright, Silas 53

Yale 43
Yell, Archibald 71
Yelobusha cotton 118
Young, Dr. Hugh 67

Zendendorf, Count 17